WEATHER AND ENERGY

BRUCE SCHWOEGLER
and
MICHAEL McCLINTOCK

An Energy Learning Systems Book
McGRAW-HILL BOOK COMPANY

New York, St. Louis, San Francisco, Auckland, Bogota, Hamburg, Johannesburg, London, Madrid,
Mexico, Montreal, New Delhi, Panama, Paris, Sao Paulo, Singapore, Sydney, Tokyo, Toronto

This book is dedicated to Barbara, Matthew, Melinda,
Marcia, Maurya, Kevin, Katie, and Liam,
with hope for an energy future free of
international tensions.

Library of Congress Cataloging in Publication Data

Schwoegler, Bruce.
  Weather and energy.

  (An Energy learning systems book)
  Bibliography: p.
  Includes index.
  1.Weather. 2.Power (Mechanics) 3.Power
resources. I.McClintock, Michael, date.
II.Title. III.Series.
QC981.45.S38   551.5   81-23671
ISBN 0-07-055746-2   AACR2

ISBN 0-07-055746-2

1234567890   KPKP   898765432

The editor for this book was Lydia Walshin, the designer and production supervisor was Dixie Clark Production. It was set in Baskerville by
Valley Composition.

(Cover photo)
A minute of lightning at Kitt Peak Observatory in Arizona. Sporadic
and of short duration, lightning is not a viable weather related source
of energy in spite of its tremendous power. One bolt produces 250 kilowatt hours of energy. Some 8 million bolts per day flash across worldwide skies approximating the daily energy consumption in the Chicago
metropolitan area.

CONTENTS

PREFACE

There is no single, simple answer to the energy problems we face today. Technologically sophisticated nations, the big users of energy, are characterized by complexity. For better or worse, one consequence of this is that the solutions to their problems are likely to be complex, too.

This book looks at the enormous amount of energy present in meteorological phenomena of all kinds. We explain how the weather system works, and explore the connections between weather and weather related sources of energy that are potentially useful. In some cases the technology that will be used to harness these sources of energy is new; in more cases it is existing technology brought up to date. In all cases the prospects are attractive because they offer energy with potentially less impact on the environment and decreased international tension. They deserve careful study and understanding, to which we hope this book will contribute.

The events of the last ten years or so have brought home a realization that inexpensive oil had prevented us from seeing: technological society is *driven* by energy. In fact, one description of energy is that it makes things happen; nothing happens without it.

The complexity of the energy issue and its importance to society compel us to explore the options seriously, carefully, and with attention to the consequences.

The sun is the major source of energy on the earth. It made coal, oil, and natural gas in the past; it makes wind, rain, and waves today. This book deals in the present. It explains how the sun's energy is changed into other forms through the interaction of the earth's atmosphere with its land and water surfaces, and how these various forms of energy can be harnessed to provide the energy people need.

The idea of developing energy sources other than the ones we now use has several important facets. Most obvious is the need to replace those resources which are in dwindling supply. There are only a few decades of oil left; experts no longer disagree about this, they merely discuss the question of timing.

All the oil wells won't simply run dry at some point in the next few decades, of course. That's not the way things work. Instead, dwindling supplies of any socially useful product without decreased demand will force higher market prices. In the present case of world oil, diminishing supply in the face of increasing demand has not only sustained higher free market prices, but also has allowed the existence of an international cartel, which causes far more rapid price rises than might otherwise occur.

So when we speak of "running out" of oil, we don't mean that one day fifty years from now we will draw the last drop of oil from the last remaining oil well with a fateful slurp, after which there will be no more. More likely, there will be such demand for the remaining supply of this resource that the price will be unbearable for all but the most exotic purposes.

Before that happens, however, substitutes will become economical. We will phase out oil (perhaps primarily because of its price, but for whatever reasons) over a period of time that actually started in the early 1970s with the oil "embargo". The rising price of oil has made it uneconomical to consider new oil-fired steam plants for generating electricity, for example — one indication that the phase-out already has begun.

There are other pressing issues as well. Today, importation of oil from foreign nations results in an outflow of United States capital to the extent of nearly 100 billion dollars a year, roughly six percent of the gross national product. To the oil exporting nations, much of this is surplus, and so a large fraction is reinvested in industry and real estate in the United States. If the world were politically more stable, this would pose little problem. In fact, it is reassuring, to a point, that the nations currently dictating the price rise of oil have a stake in our economy, since their stake acts as a check on oil prices.

Of course, the world is not politically stable; and as we have recently seen in Iran, large amounts of capital in the hands of an unstable political regime can be an unsettling influence in the world. The oil consuming nations of the world are vulnerable if they continue to think in terms of oil as the primary source of energy. But we can become less vulnerable and can assist the developing nations at the same time if we think more creatively and use the time available to develop better energy sources.

What we are saying, then, is that political as well as economic factors play an important part in the current energy problems of the world, not just of the United States.

A necessary ingredient to energy solutions in the United States, therefore, is the development not just of alternative sources, but of domestic alternatives, as far as possible. Domestic energy sources not only would decrease the outflow of United States capital to politically unstable areas of the world, but it would also create domestic employment.

Given the present complex situation, which energy sources shall we develop? It is neither the purpose of this book to advocate one group of energy sources over another, nor to be a definitive meteorological text. It is not difficult, however, for us to spell out some criteria that must be satisfied by any new sources we consider.

First, these new sources must provide energy economically. This means they must either be competitive with traditional energy sources or they must be made so by government subsidy. Presently oil is heavily subsidized in the United States, so this poses no particular problem of precedent. In fact, some people claim that if the subsidies were removed from presently subsidized sources, then better sources would be economical already.

Second, the new energy sources must be environmentally acceptable. A major need, for example, is a significant energy source that does not add to the atmospheric content of carbon dioxide. We have reached a point in our consumption of energy where the burning of fossil fuels is changing the atmosphere's composition enough to cause foreseeable changes in climate. Chapter 7 explains how this happens, and why the group of weather related sources of energy fulfill the requirments for energy that will reverse the present trend. Though we have a bit more to say here about environmental consequences, there is a great body of literature available on the subject, so we have not attempted an exhaustive treatment. Environmental acceptability is obviously a requirement, however, and deserves careful consideration by a society interested in long-term existence.

Third, there must be enough energy in the proposed alternative sources to be useful. It would be of little use to spend time and money developing energy sources which would get us through only the next twenty years. Here, of course, some of the renewable alternatives come into their own (recurrent may be a more precise word, since some are self-renewing). As you will see in this book, not only is there enormous energy in meteorological phenomena, but also this energy recurs with predictable regularity, and in that sense it is often regarded as an inexhaustible supply.

Fourth, the new energy sources should be domestic, and here many of the weather related phenomena do especially well, for every country in the world has some share of weather. In fact some sources, like direct solar energy, already are distributed among the nations of the world in appropriately useful amounts, so that an extensive distribution network is not necessary.

Fifth, labor intensive sources are preferable to capital intensive ones. The need for employment could be met, and a reduced need for capital would ease the present capital shortage in the United States and in the world.

Energy conservation as a "source" of energy satisfies all of these requirements, and should be pursued vigorously at the outset. We do not treat this subject directly in the present book; there is a growing body of literature on the subject for the interested reader. For example, Stobaugh and Yergin of the Harvard Business School have spoken eloquently on this subject in their book, *Energy Future*. Conservation as an energy "source" can buy developed nations the time needed to develop new sources.

But conservation is little help to underdeveloped nations that require energy for their development; they don't use any to conserve on. So the next obvious need is for energy sources that contribute to supply rather than, like conservation, reduce demand.

Each of the authors, as a member of his own professional discipline, is painfully conscious of two things: the abridgement of material in our respective disciplines in order to produce this brief book, and the gratitude we owe to our scientific colleagues on whose work we have drawn extensively. We hope specialists in each of the areas we have touched on will forgive our all too brief treatment of their areas of interest, and we thank them for their contributions to the literature that have made this book possible.

Our warm thanks go to Barbara and Marcia for providing encouragement and understanding during the development of this book. Special thanks are due to Harry and Ginger Jones of Vineyard Haven and to Tom Roche of Killington for generously providing a hospitable environment that allowed writing of the manuscript.

We would like to thank Bob Entwistle for bringing the co-authors of this book together, and for his continuing encouragement and enthusiasm during the progress of its development. Thanks are also due to Dixie Clark for excellent production, to Lydia Walshin for her expert editorial assistance, and to Nancy Benson for her patient deciphering of our handscript and typing of several versions of the manuscript.

Finally, the co-authors would like to thank each other for what has turned out to be a most productive collaboration.

BWS, MM

ABOUT
THE AUTHORS

Bruce Schwoegler is with WBZ radio and television in Boston, Massachusetts, where he is a weather forecaster, science reporter, and producer and host of a series of energy specials. The former naval officer is also an environmental consultant, science lecturer, meteorology instructor, and author of magazine articles on the weather. Mr. Schwoegler received a B.S. degree from the University of Wisconsin, where he majored in naval science and meteorology.

Michael McClintock is the president of Michael McClintock and Associates, an energy consulting firm in Boston, Massachusetts. He is a specialist in energy conservation and solar energy and presently is committed to the development of new solar energy systems. In addition, he has wide experience in the communication of innovative ideas through writing, lecturing, teaching, and consulting. Dr. McClintock received a B.S. degree in engineering from the University of Arizona, an M.S. degree in physics and an M.S. degree in engineering from the University of Colorado, and a Ph.D. in physics from the University of Colorado. He is a registered professional engineer in Massachusetts and Colorado.

1

THE GREAT BLIZZARD OF 1978

Sunday, February 5, 1978. Four hundred miles south of New England and just east of Cape Hatteras, North Carolina, mild and humid air lingers over the area, with attendant showers and thunderstorms. Below, the warm waters of the Gulf Stream are rushing northward, warming and humidfying the air layer immediately above the ocean.

A thousand miles west of this damp marine environment, shivering passengers boarding planes in Chicago hear optimistic reports from the pilots for a fast trip to Tampa and Miami. High-speed winds in the upper atmosphere are plunging southward, creating advantageous tailwinds, so the trip will be shorter than usual. But these tailwinds also are pushing cold air deep into the South.

Meteorologists throughout the Northeast are studying their charts closely. They know that strong winds, mild and humid air, and frigid air in close proximity to each other might

1

trigger a really explosive weather situation. That night, the giant computers of the National Weather Service point the finger at New England. One of the things a computer can do well is assimilate the data from hundreds of meteorological measurements, process them, and turn them into a forecast — a major storm is about to develop.

Monday, February 6, 1978, finds the developing storm some 200 miles south of New England and closing fast. Heavy snow is falling in New York City. On Cape Cod, winds are gusting to hurricane force. Sand-spitting waves blast the coast, and the worst truly is yet to come.

The snow falls faster than plows can clear it from major roads, and the wind undoes the work of the plows just a few feet behind them anyway. The unusually high tide caused by the storm's occurring at full moon is even higher along the Atlantic seacoast, because of the very low atmospheric pressure in the center of the storm. Figure 1-1. With high winds driving huge waves against the shores, even the sheltered harbor of Boston, as well as its north and south coasts, is severely damaged.

Two days later New England digs out from what clearly has been the storm of the century. Hurricane winds and seas combined with very high tides have devastated a large section of the coast. Massachusetts, Connecticut, and Rhode Island are declared federal disaster areas. Two of the region's largest cities, Providence and Boston, are paralyzed. Thousands of cars lie buried in mile-long rows beneath snowdrifts on New England highways.

The Great Blizzard of 1978 killed, displaced, stranded, and inconvenienced people from New Jersey to Maine. Total cost: approximately one billion dollars. The storm was one of the ten worst disasters in the history of the United States.

After the blowing snow, sea spray, and resulting personal hardships passed, we were left with an impression of fundamental importance: the atmosphere had shown us its tremendous power and the energy it can unleash. In fact, the Blizzard of 1978 was a three-day storm with enough energy to power the entire country for several months!

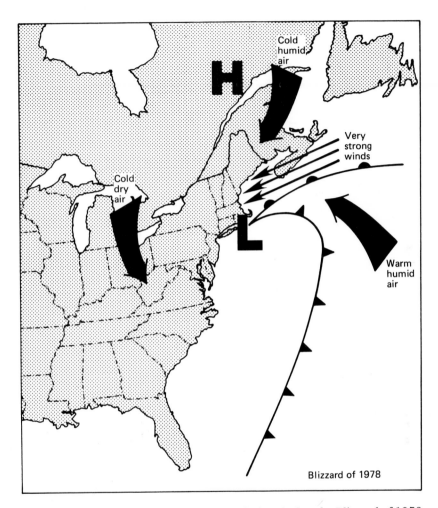

Figure 1-1   Weather systems and circulation during the Blizzard of 1978

There is an awesome amount of energy in atmospheric phenomena, and it's particularly awesome when we experience the destructive force of a storm at close hand. There is even more energy in sunshine, though we don't see it as vividly because it is released less suddenly and less locally. Some fraction of all this energy in the Earth's sun/atmosphere system is potentially useful for practical purposes. The total amount of energy is so large that even a small fraction would suffice for the foreseeable future.

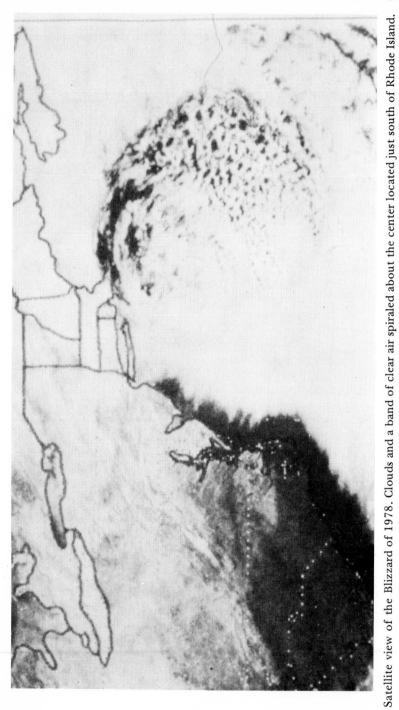

Satellite view of the Blizzard of 1978. Clouds and a band of clear air spiraled about the center located just south of Rhode Island.

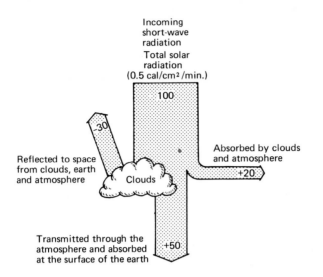

Figure 1-2 Graphic representation of the average energy budget for a yearly period. Energy reaching the top of Earth's atmosphere from the sun is assigned a value of 100 units. On an annual basis, the planet is neither heating nor cooling since a total of 70 units of the incoming energy is absorbed, and the same amount is re-radiated into space.

If we were to compare the energy in an atmospheric disturbance (like the storm of 1978) with the frequency of occurrence, we would find that the storms with the greatest energy content occur least frequently, and that the frequency of occurrence increases as the energy decreases.

Though it is tempting from an energy standpoint to look enviously at the storms with the most energy content, it is unlikely that they are of practical value. The reason is economic. In order to build a system, — a windmill, perhaps — that would produce power without destroying itself in such a storm, the capital investment would be too great for the few times it would be in a position to produce.

Furthermore, in the course of a year, the energy retrievable from a few big storms is less than that from less energetic phenomena which occur more frequently. This then leads to a sensible strategy. For a given approach to energy capture, we can note the useful energy that will be produced by machines of various size and cost over a year, and build the economic optimum. We will talk about this in greater detail in Chapter 8.

The energy in the weather comes from the sun. Figure 1-2 shows how the earth distributes among several energy forms the radiation it gets from the sun. We will explore these energy forms in detail in later chapters. Also, although energy is released in the earth's atmosphere at various heights, we will be most interested in the energy at or very near the surface. We will also see how to use this energy that exists near the surface for practical purposes, and what effect variations in the weather have on this practical use.

2

GLOBAL CIRCULATION

Every day, everywhere in the world, the kinetic energy of motion is present in the atmosphere and in the seas. Most of this energy is not explosive or destructive, as was the Great Blizzard of 1978; rather it is constantly expanding and evolving, like the push of the wind, the roll of the sea, the current in a rain-swollen river, or the heat of the sun. All can provide the energy people need.

Earth occupies an ideal position in the solar system: just the right distance from the sun to receive the radiation necessary for life to flourish. Racing about the sun, our planet follows an elliptical orbit that takes us farthest from the sun during summer (aphelion, 94.5 million miles) and closest to it in winter (perihelion, 91.4 millon miles). Ironically, the 3.1-million-mile difference actually gives us more sunshine during the cold season (7 percent) in the Northern Hemisphere, and less radiation during the warm season. The *tilt* of the planet's axis (23.5 degrees) determines the changing seasons, not the

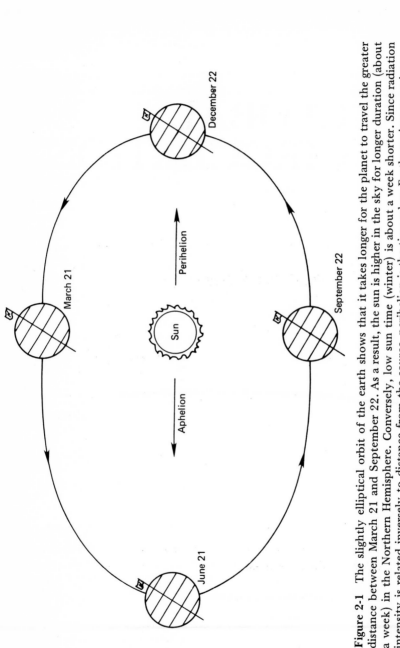

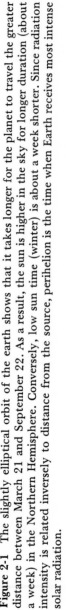

Figure 2-1 The slightly elliptical orbit of the earth shows that it takes longer for the planet to travel the greater distance between March 21 and September 22. As a result, the sun is higher in the sky for longer duration (about a week) in the Northern Hemisphere. Conversely, low sun time (winter) is about a week shorter. Since radiation intensity is related inversely to distance from the source, perihelion is the time when Earth receives most intense solar radiation.

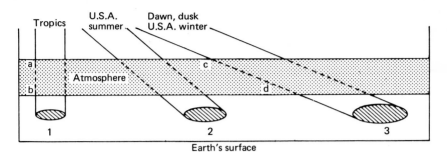

Figure 2-2　Spreading of solar energy as in a flashlight beam is illustrated positions 1, 2, and 3. Spreading is evident with changing seasons and at dawn and dusk. Passage through atmosphere further weakens and scatters the beam, especially at c-d, and is more pronounced in polluted air.

overall radiation received (Figure 2-1). Were the Northern Hemisphere tilted toward the sun at perihelion, temperature extremes would be more severe and larger areas of our hemisphere would be uninhabitable.

Solar rays penetrate the atmosphere like a flashlight beam penetrates a dusty room, arriving at the earth's surface both as beam and as diffuse (scattered) radiation. Diffuse radiation would be like the faint tracing of the beam in the room's dusty air; it would throw a glow on a distant wall surrounding the brilliant circle illuminated by the direct beam itself. The beam's passage through the atmosphere is longer in the hemisphere tilted away from the sun (Figure 2-2). The greater distance the beam has to travel saps its strength as more particles intercept it, absorbing its energy and producing more diffuse and scattered radiation.

In other words, particles in the atmosphere interact with the incoming solar radiation. The sky is blue because the atmosphere scatters blue light more strongly in these interactions. At sunset, the greater distance through the atmosphere a beam has to travel weakens it, so you can look directly at the sun. You also can see that the sky is no longer the same color blue as at midday; this is because solar rays coming in at a lower angle interact with more of the atmosphere. Indeed, the sky color is different at midday in winter than in summer, when the sun is more nearly vertical and the rays more direct.

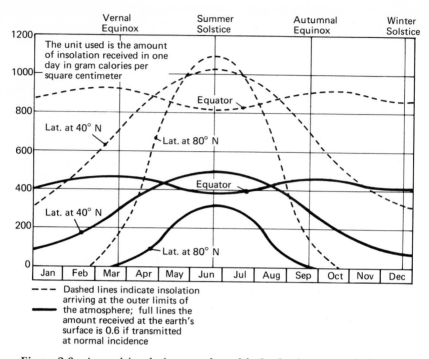

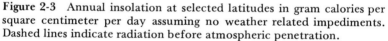

Figure 2-3 Annual insolation at selected latitudes in gram calories per square centimeter per day assuming no weather related impediments. Dashed lines indicate radiation before atmospheric penetration.

At noon in the tropics, a nearly vertical sun passes overhead. From the equator northward to Florida, a distance of approximately 1,800 miles, this solar radiation girdles the earth, falling mostly on ocean waters. Throughout the seasons, the sun's rays are most direct at these tropical latitudes, where they strike the earth with little deviation from the vertical. Farther north and south, the parallel beams of light strike the earth more obliquely (Figure 2-2) and vary with the seasons, thus decreasing the intensity of the radiation beam (Figure 2-3). A surplus of solar energy falls at tropical locations, whereas at latitudes more distant from the equator, the earth loses more energy to space, on the average, than it receives from the sun (Figure 2-4).

There are primarily two reasons for this: First, in the polar regions the solar rays coming in are less intense than the radi-

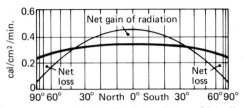

Figure 2-4 Average annual latitudinal insolation (thin line) and terrestrial radiation (thick line). Atmosphere motions result when zones of net gain and net loss seek equilibrium.

ation loss out from the earth's surface at these latitudes. Second, in the equatorial regions, humid, tropical air tends to block heat loss from the earth's surface, like the glass in a greenhouse. The result? Steambath tropics and deep-freeze poles which continually interact through circulation patterns (wind) in the atmosphere in an attempt to equalize the temperatures of these unequally heated regions. So, the sun's shining as it does in one part of the world makes the wind blow in another.

Tropical solar radiation strikes both land and water and warms both. The warmer surfaces, like stove elements heating a pan, transfer their heat to the air immediately above by a process called *conduction*. Because heat always flows from a warmer object to a colder one, conduction is a most effective heat transfer process. When you hold an ice cube in your hand, the numbing and pain you feel is caused by heat conduction from your hand to the ice. The greater the temperature difference between two objects, the faster the heat is transferred. When heated by conduction, air rises, lifting warmer air to greater heights by *convection*, the process which distributes heat vertically in the atmosphere.

At night, warm water and land continue to warm the nearby air as they cool off. Water cools more slowly than land, because land is heated only in its uppermost layers, while water mixes its acquired heat, storing it throughout a greater depth. The heat from the earth, seeking cooler locales, radiates into the nighttime sky, giving off infrared radiation in the process. If you sit in front of a fireplace filled with glowing embers, you feel warmth as infrared radiation strikes your body; air, too, feels this warming, particularly if it is moist. Humid air absorbs infrared radiation, blocking its escape to space, but dry air absorbs much less. This loss of heat, radiational cooling, is severe in dry climates such as deserts. Humid Miami at 85°F may experience radiational cooling to a nighttime temperature of 65°F, while dry Phoenix may see a temperature drop from 90 to 45°F. The world's deserts are known for this hostile temperature differential.

Tepid tropical waters and breezes exhibit what is called sensible heat, (that accompanied by a change in temperature) but a more important form of heat acquired in the tropics is that part of the sun's energy (one-fourth of the total striking earth) which makes water evaporate and suspends it in the atmosphere. This water vapor, liberated to the air, represents roughly 1,000 billion tons of water molecules packed with what is called *latent heat of vaporization*. Released into the skies each day, this broad flow of warm, humid, tropical air rises and migrates toward mid-latitudes. Like a genie in a bottle, the hidden (latent) energy is waiting to be rubbed by the colder air of the northern latitudes. This is the situation that provided the energy to ignite the Great Blizzard of 1978.

The theory of global circulation is complex, but if you know the basics you will understand the relation between weather and energy. Briefly stated, the atmosphere of the earth contains warm, humid air which rises and flows from the tropics toward the poles (Figure 2-5). A replenishing airflow completes the cycle, in which cold air, since it is more dense, moves from the poles at lower altitude toward the equator. Throughout their cyclic journey these air flows travel over mountain ranges, seas, and continents below, and ride a roller coaster created by local variations in heating and cooling.

When air is warmed it expands, becomes less dense than surrounding air, and rises: the principle on which a hot air ballon operates. When air is cooled, it contracts and becomes more dense, sinking to the region just above the earth's surface. These vertical motions are the key to understanding the pressure systems to which meteorologists refer: *low pressure areas* are regions of less dense air on the rise; *high pressure areas* are regions of denser air that is falling. Extended to planetary scale, in our circulation model (Figure 2-5) we have

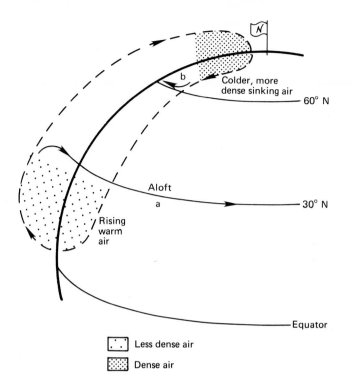

Figure 2-5 A simplified picture of the earth's atmospheric circulation. Air is heated at the equator where it rises and migrates northward. Cooled in the polar regions, the air becomes more dense, sinks to lower altitude, and returns to the equator. (Points a and b represent new air-flow directions after consideration for Coriolis force, discussed later in this section).

broad areas of sinking cold air at the poles (high pressure) and warm air rising near the equator (low pressure). Like hissing air escaping from an inflated tire, the air from a high pressure area rushes to fill a low pressure area. In just this way, polar high pressure air seeking tropical regions of lower pressure contributed to the fury of the Great Blizzard of 1978. It was this cold hand that sprung the energetic genie from the bottle.

If the earth did not rotate, the overall global circulation pattern would not differ greatly from our simplified model.

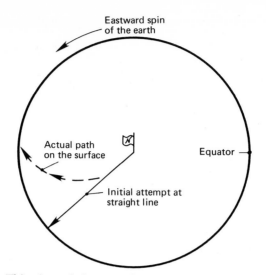

Figure 2-6 This view of the top of the Earth is analogous to a record on a turntable. The rotating planet (record) causes an initial attempt at drawing a straight line to curve instead, to the right. This deflection is called the coriolis force.

But direct north-to-south airflow will not occur over a rotating surface. To understand why, imagine that you are located at the center of a record turntable. Call this the North Pole; the rim of the record is analogous to the equator. If the record spins counterclockwise, as the earth would appear to rotate from a vantage point above the North Pole, the equator would move much faster than the pole area (Figure 2-6). In fact, at our location near the center of the record very little motion would occur; the rim would travel considerably faster at the edge of the turntable.

Now, if we try to draw a straight line at constant pen speed from the center of a spinning record to its rim, imitating the proposed airflow from north to south, the result will be a line that curves to the right on the surface of the record. The attempt to connect the center and a rim point with a straight line has failed because the rim point is racing rapidly to the east, and by the time we near the finish of our experiment, the rim has left the pencil behind. Viewed from the vantage point of the earth (the record), it would appear that an unseen force has been pushing us to the right. This apparent force is called the *coriolis force* and it affects all objects moving through the atmosphere. A plane flying from Maine to Miami must compensate for this effect or it would land in Mexico, just as our line missed the original target point on the rim of the record.

Flowing air and water masses experience the same effect; the coriolis force causes moving air to curve to the right in the Northern Hemisphere, although the analogy is imperfect because the coriolis force is actually caused by conservation of the angular momentum of an air mass as it moves toward or away from the earth's axis of rotation in its northward or southward flow.

Relating this rule to the global circulation model, note that high level air moving north from the tropics curves to the right, or east. Lower level polar air moving south curves to the right, or west. (See Figure 2-5). In the first case, airflow curvature is most evident at about 30°, and the wind blows predominantly from the west. But in the northward, curving journey, the upper level winds have cooled, piled into each other, and begun to sink. Therefore, at this latitude (including North Florida) winds aloft are from the west and cool air is sinking — a high pressure indicator. Florida, the "Sunshine State", epitomizes the fair weather regime of this zone.

The sinking air spreads out as it approaches ground level. Part of it returns to the tropics to be heated and lifted again. Its coriolis-induced trajectory creates a generally east-to-west motion; these are the northeasterly tradewinds favored by mariners sailing to the New World long ago. The other outflow, of greater depth, moves northward and curves to the right, becoming west winds. These are the prevailing westerlies, the dominant airflow above and across the United States. Continuing around the globe at mid-latitude, they provide the driving force for sailors returning to the European continent (Figure 2-7). Note that winds are named for the direction *from* which they blow.

The northern boundary of the westerlies is a zone where colder air from the north meets and interacts with the west winds. Between the poles and 60° (northern Canada), polar air heads southward at lower levels and, curving to the right or west, becomes the polar easterlies. Converging east and

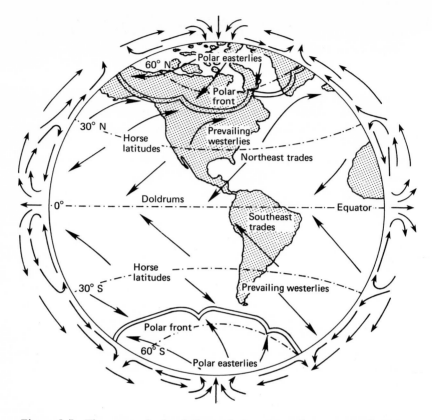

Figure 2-7 The general circulation of the atmosphere approximates the global winds pictured here. The complex airflow transports heat from the equator to the deficient poles. Note the gear-like appearance of the vertical cross section. Combined with the effects of the earth's rotation, bands of winds are generated and carry familiar names such as the prevailing Westerlies.

west airflows have nowhere to go but up, so the milder, less dense westerlies are forced aloft. As we discussed earlier, this is a low pressure zone characterized by rising, cooling air and frequent cloudy weather. Named the Polar Front, it is the spawning ground for the organized lows called *storms* that gather energy and race across the United States and Canada.

In winter the colder surface polar air breaks out spasmodically to locations farther south. Since the lifting of the mild air also occurs farther south, the low pressure zone and the storms associated with it then tend to develop at more southerly locations. The paths they follow after their formation are called *storm tracks*. These tracks migrate with the seasons, as do the westerlies, moving north during the summer and farther south during the winter when less solar radiation falls in the north polar region. This causes the cold polar air to plunge to its lowest temperatures and latitudes.

The cloudiness and storminess associated with storm tracks raise important questions about the application of alternative energy. Is solar energy a viable alternative in a generally cloudy location? Where might wind energy be a better solution? As you can see, answers to questions of practical significance are beginning to unfold even from this simplified model of our planet's atmospheric mechanism.

Let's recap our discussion. Warm and humid air flows generally northward from the tropics at higher levels, and sinks in a high pressure zone near 30° latitude. It spreads in two directions, part returning to the tropics and part heading northward. The latter part becomes a mild, prevailing westerly wind between 30 and 60°, and at the northern boundary this air stream is forced upward by the cold, polar, easterly winds. This zone of rising air, characterized by low pressure, is the birthplace of most weather affecting the United States. It is believed that the lifted air spreads out at the upper levels with most returning to the pole and some heading southward. The planetary airflow and embedded weather systems transfer energy from one to another, almost like a gear train; the excess energy of the tropics is thus ultimately transferred in several steps to the energy-deficient polar regions, and it is this complex process that generates weather, the earth's atmosphere in motion. Complete planetary circulation is shown in cross-section in Figure 2-7, but is oversimplified, and a more complete treatment is available in the references.

We should note that diagrams like Figure 2-7 distort the scale of events rather badly. The earth's atmosphere is not nearly as thick as it appears in the diagram. Most of it lies below the altitude of the highest point on Mt. Everest, which is roughly six miles above sea level, whereas the earth's diameter is approximately 8,000 miles. If the atmosphere were repre-

This satellite picture of September weather reveals unsettled conditions girdling tropical locales. Note the hurricane churning in the Pacific Ocean off Baja California. Farther north, more cloudiness is present as Polar air does battle in the vicinity of 60 degrees north latitude.

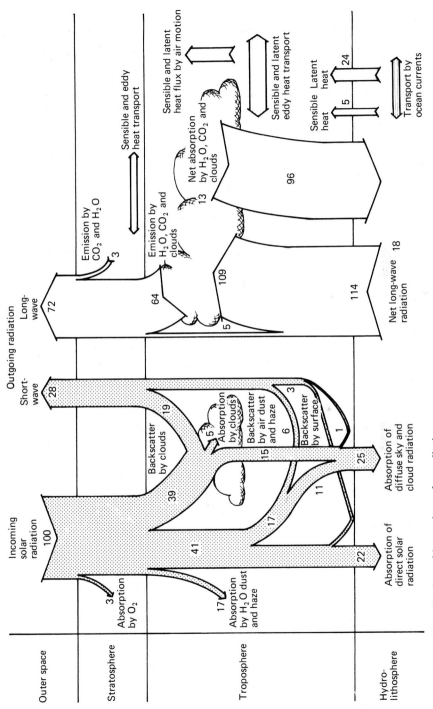

Figure 2-8 Distribution of incoming solar radiation.

sented to scale on a sixteen-inch globe, it would therefore be approximately one-eightieth of an inch deep, roughly the thickness of two sheets of paper. Since the straight line distance over the surface of the earth from the equator to 30° is roughly 1,800 nautical miles, each of the atmospheric circulation zones in its extent from north to south is several hundred times the depth.

The sun shining makes the wind blow. The circulation pattern of the wind is the atmosphere's response to uneven solar heating of the planet, its attempt to establish temperature equilibrium. More sunshine strikes the equatorial regions, and less strikes the higher latitudes toward both poles. The atmosphere's response is rising air in the lower latitudes which are heated most strongly by the sun; a migration of this air poleward; and descending air in the polar regions that moves toward the equator to replace the poleward flowing air.

On a global scale, the incoming energy from the sun is handled by the earth as shown in Figure 2-8. Of 100 percent incoming solar radiation, approximately 28 percent is reflected back into space immediately by clouds, dust, and the surface of the earth. The remaining 72 percent enters the atmospheric system where it is absorbed and scattered by various processes, and interactions of the atmosphere-ocean system. Three percent, in the ultraviolet spectrum, is absorbed in the stratosphere; 17 percent is absorbed by water vapor, dust, and haze in the lower atmosphere; and 47 percent is absorbed by either surface water or land, some of this after being scattered into diffuse radiation by clouds and other atmospheric constituents.

Figure 2-9 shows the energy distribution from another point of view, one which suggests the possibility of practical use of some of this energy. For example, we can see that the total power in winds, waves, convection (vertical atmospheric motion), and currents is some 0.2 percent of the solar energy received by the earth, and amounts to 370 million million watts (370×10^{12} watts). For our purposes it is useful to compare the weather related energy forms with present energy usage, and we will do so occasionally in this book.

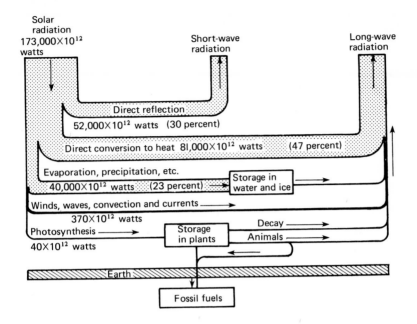

Figure 2-9 Flow of energy to and from the earth is depicted by means of bands and lines that suggest by their width the contribution of each item to the earth's energy budget. The principal inputs are solar radiation, tidal energy and the energy from nuclear, thermal and gravitational sources. More than 99 percent of the input is solar radiation. The apportionment of incoming solar radiation is indicated by the horizontal bands beginning with "Direct reflection" and reading downward. The smallest portion goes to photosynthesis. Dead plants and animals buried in the earth give rise to fossil fuels, containing stored solar energy from millions of years past.

Three hundred and seventy million million watts is approximately one thousand times the electrical generating capacity in the United States, and the energy in these processes over the course of a year is some thirty-seven times the world's use of energy in 1979, so clearly there is enough energy involved in these processes to merit our consideration for possible practical application. We will refer back to Figure 2-9 occasionally throughout our discussions.

In the following chapters we will concern ourselves largely with the geographic area of the earth from 30 to 60° N, the mid-northern latitudes. The greater part of the North American landmass lies between these latitudes and beneath the sea of air we call the atmosphere. The weather in this "sea" affects our lives in numerous ways, and also can be used to our advantage.

3

MOISTURE AND CLOUDS

Looking at clouds "from both sides now" has heretofore been the prerogative of Judy Collins and airline travelers. Weather satellites are expanding the vista. Understanding the physics of clouds increases the appreciation of their multidimensional aspects and contribution to the weather machine. Puffy, peculiar or precipitating clouds are a manifestation of atmospheric dynamics. What are they? What do they mean?

Clouds are not just airy drifters in the sky. They are packaged energy, water weighted messengers and solar reflectors. One white fluff in a blue sky can weigh a half million tons; one thunderstorm weighs several million tons! Just the energy involved in raising this weight of water to 10,000 feet is impressive: the equivalent in hydroelectric potential of roughly two million kilowatt hours. In addition, the latent heat of vaporization accounts for some 150 times this amount of energy.

Clouds, which you can see, and water vapor, which you can't see, are two ways the atmosphere carries moisture around. Clouds vary in shape and size, giving us clues to the coming weather; but water vapor can be seen only when it is clothed in a developing cloud, or when it cools, changes state, and becomes a liquid through the process of condensation.

Moisture in the air represents a tremendous source of energy, and under certain circumstances this can be released to power the atmospheric motions. Clouds are not only a manifestation of weather, they also affect the weather by changing the amount of sunshine that gets to the surface. Fog, especially regularly occurring fog in a particular location, modifies the sunshine reaching the ground or a solar installation. And moisture in the air in all of these forms is part of the hydrological cycle that among other things, allows the production of hydroelectric power.

Therefore, an understanding of the energetic and the optical effects of moisture in the air, as well as the terminology and some of the more direct manifestations of moisture are important to our later purpose in this book.

Water vapor and clouds are the same basic H_2O, of course. From a physical point of view the change of phase between the two states merely represents a different degree of molecular aggregation. In the liquid, a large number of water molecules are close enough to each other to maintain a kind of "contact." Adding heat to the liquid provides some molecules with enough energy to break away, and these "free" water molecules make up the vapor.

The process works both ways: when molecules in the vapor condense to form the liquid, heat is released (latent heat of condensation). Figure 3-1 illustrates the heat content of a pound of water as the temperature changes. Moisture-laden air represents a tremendous amount of traveling atmospheric energy. When any part of the air mass is cooled to the dew point, the energy of condensation is released. This higher energy part of the air mass is then unstable with respect to the rest, and the sudden release of energy increases the motion of the air mass in some way.

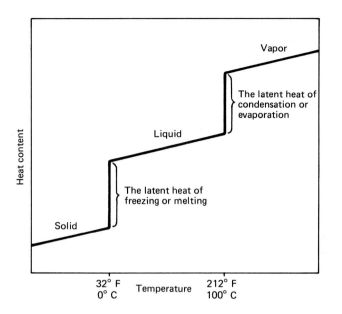

Figure 3-1 The heat content of water. As heat is added, the temperature increases until a temperature is reached where a change of phase takes place. At these temperatures the heat content changes drastically with no change in temperature until the water is in the new phase.

There is often more than a thousand times more energy in humid air as latent heat than is contained in the same air as wind. An average thunderstorm releases roughly 500 million kilowatt hours of energy through the condensation of water. This is as much energy as a town of 30,000 people uses in a year.

The evaporation of water (by solar energy), transport of the vapor into the atmosphere, condensation, and eventual precipitation make up the *hydrological cycle*. In the mid-latitudes of the earth, these processes transport roughly 23 to 33 percent of the heat from tropical regions toward the poles. The remainder is transported in the form of sensible heat (44 percent) and by ocean currents (33 percent).

The most impressive aspect of the hydrological cycle is the enormous amount of energy represented by the latent heat of condensation of water from vapor to liquid.

Condensation plays another important part in the weather: it helps control the temperature of the earth. When more solar energy gets through to the surface of the earth, more water evaporates from the oceans, creating a cloudier atmosphere which in turn blocks the sunshine and its energy from getting to the earth.

We haven't yet answered the question of why water vapor is invisible and clouds are visible. There is water vapor in the air you breathe, of course, but you still can see across the room clearly.

The answer is merely in the size of the molecular aggregation. Particles small with respect to the wavelength of light do not scatter light, so we cannot see them. It takes a particle whose size is comparable to, or larger than, the wavelength of light to be visible, so what you "see" in a cloud is not water vapor itself but really condensed droplets of water. In the case of water molecules a droplet must contain at least 10 billion or so molecules to be visible.

In vapor form, water is transparent to visible light although it absorbs infrared radiation for another reason. Water vapor, therefore, plays an important part in the "greenhouse effect" of the planet's atmosphere (See Chapter 7) but condensed water drops — clouds — also play a large part in the reflection of solar energy and the energy balance of the earth.

Air at a given pressure and temperature can hold only so much water vapor. Imagine a room full of people, representing moist air in a container at a given temperature, with the people themselves representing the water vapor in the air. If the room is filled with people, we say that the air is saturated; it holds 100 percent of what it is capable of holding, corresponding to 100 percent relative humidity (RH) (Figure 3-2(a)).

For each approximate 18° F increase in the air temperature, the room (the air) can hold twice as much water vapor. In the analogy, we double the size of the room, but let in no people; 50 percent of the room is now empty (Figure 3-2(b)). Adding another 18°F doubles the room size again; but if we add no people, then only one-fourth (25 percent) of the

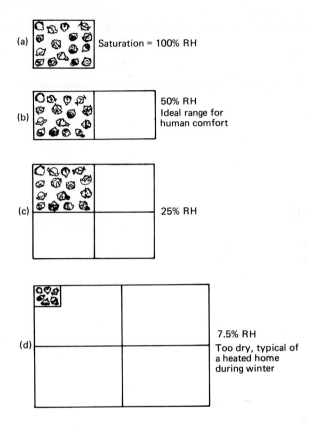

Figure 3-2 A roomful of relatives viewed from above

room is occupied (Figure 3-2(c)). Warmer air can hold more water vapor.

This relationship between water vapor (people) and air temperature (room size) works both ways. Note that for each 18° F *decrease* in the temperature, the room size decreases by one-half, doubling the relative humidity. But the maximum relative humidity (100 percent) is the condition in which the room is filled (saturated). The temperature of the air at this saturation level is called the *dew point*, the temperature at which condensation begins because the air can hold no more water as vapor. Air can be cooled to the dew point but rarely below it without condensation; if we chill the air further, people must be forced out of the room by the cooling.

If air is cooled to its dewpoint by an object which is below freezing, frost forms as on this twig.

Continued cooling results in both temperature and dew point falling together, and condensation continues. Air conditioning units drip water because hot, humid air 90° F, for example, with a dew point of 70° F, is chilled to 60° F. From 90° F to 70° F, no moisture is produced; but from saturation at 70° F, condensation occurs continually as both temperature and dew point fall. Dehumidifiers wring moisture from the air in a similar manner.

Cooling moist air to the dew point with a cold solid object coats the object with dew, for example, the "sweat" on a drinking glass or the early morning beads of moisture on blades of grass or a car body.

Meteorologists prefer the term "dew point temperature" to "relative humidity" when describing humidity, since the relative humidity varies with the temperature of an air mass, though the moisture content may remain the same. In the cool of the morning, the relative humidity might be 100 percent, but daytime heating might cause it to fall to 30 percent, though the dew point remained unchanged.

However, relative humidity is a useful concept, especially during winter, and it has significant applications in energy use and health. For example, if you step out of a warm shower on a cold, dry winter day, even in a well-heated room, you can get quite a chill if the air in the room is extremely dry. Here's why: Consider outside air at 60 percent RH and 20°F. Remember that heating the air halves the relative humidity for each 18° temperature increment. So bringing that air into a room at 74°F would give it a desert-dry humidity of 7.5 percent. (74 – 20 = 54, or 3 eighteen-degree increments, so halving 60 percent three times equals 7.5 percent RH). This very low RH means that the air is receptive to much more water vapor; in other words, a large room with few people is an invitation to more people to join the party (Figure 3-2(d)). Water droplets on the skin evaporate more readily, stealing the heat required for evaporation from the body, and become water vapor in the air.

This evaporative cooling makes your body feel colder than expected in 74°F temperature. A home should be humidified to between 30 and 50 percent RH during very cold weather, not only to lessen this chill, but also to moisturize skin tissue, particularly in the nasal passages. This is believed to help prevent disease; since dried membranes cannot filter inhaled air, disease-carrying organisms can travel deeper into the respiratory tract.

Evaporative cooling of the body also contributes to wind chill outdoors, although a greater contributor to outdoor chilling is the wind itself, which strips away the static layer of warmer air just above the surface of the skin. Colder air, whether dry or humid, conducts heat away from the body more rapidly, so the combination of low air temperature, low RH, and high wind speed produces more severe wind chill effects. As a practical matter, evaporative cooling can be helpful in the Southwest where hot air with low relative humidity in the summertime is very receptive to evaporation; evaporative cooling makes the extreme heat more tolerable to individuals.

Heat from hot, dry air can be "stolen," by evaporating water to produce cooler air at a higher relative humidity. This evaporative air conditioning process uses less energy, since the evaporation of water does a lot of the cooling a normal air conditioning system otherwise would do. So this kind of air conditioning makes good energy sense for dry climates, assuming no shortage of ground water.

When the atmosphere away from any object is cooled to the dew point, condensation probably will take place and millions of droplets will form a cloud. In this process, water vapor gathers around a condensation nucleus, which may be a fleck of dust, a speck of sea salt, or any of the numerous particles floating in the atmosphere. Salt is adept at grabbing moisture, which is why salt shakers clog on humid summer days. This hygroscopic property enhances accretion (massing) of water vapor even before the dew point is reached, producing familiar seaside haze. "Dirty" air in coal burning England a century ago not only caused health problems, but also produced lingering fog and haze with more dense accretions culminating in "pea soupers."

Fog is a ground based cloud which can form in several ways. For example, cool, moist air flowing over colder water off the California coast is chilled by the surface waters. If the air is chilled to the dew point, large fog banks develop (Figure 3-3). Fog also forms when moist, tropical air flows northward over colder seas. The Grand Banks off the northeast coast of the United States experience these ship killers as moist air from the south flows to that region. The nearby Gulf Stream ensures a continued supply of mild, humid air.

Sea fogs may move inland with the general flow of air around highs or lows, or they may be drawn inland by a sea breeze (onshore wind) and remain overnight or longer. These fogs are especially common during the spring when northern seas and landmasses are still cold. Sea breezes and hitch-hiking fogs are discussed in greater detail in Chapters 6 and 8.

Onshore winds also can contribute to fog formation in a different way. For example, the normal air flow from the Gulf of Mexico or Florida sea breezes draw moist air inland. If there are clear nighttime skies and light winds, the rapidly cooling land soon reaches the dew point temperature of this traveling sea air, and fog forms (Figure 3-4). It is especially thick near valleys, swamps, rivers, and lakes, where moisture is already plentiful and cold air has sunk to the low levels afforded by these terrain features. This nighttime ground

Fog banks along the California coast.

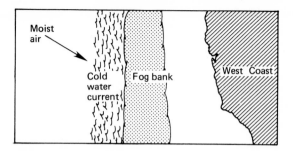

Figure 3-3 Air, cooled to the dewpoint by cold California coastal waters, becomes foggy as it approaches the coast.

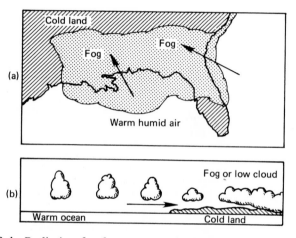

Figure 3-4 Radiation fog forms across the South when moist air moves inland from nearby waters and experiences nighttime radiational cooling to its dewpoint. The fog burns off the following morning as the rising sun heats the air to temperatures above the dewpoint.

fog is called *radiation fog*, since nighttime radiational cooling is mainly responsible for its development.

Falling rain humidifies the air it passes through, which increases the dew point temperature and also causes fog to form. Note that in all these cases of fog, the air temperature and dew point readings approach the same value; when they are the same, this indicates saturation (100 percent RH). When these two indicators are far apart, they describe dry air. The numerical difference between the two readings indicates the likelihood of fog formation or dissipation.

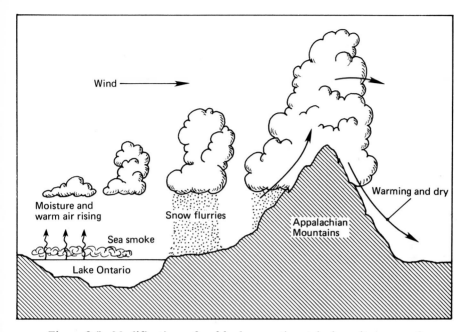

Figure 3-5 Modification of cold, dry continental air as it crosses the Great Lakes

Mixing cold air with moist, mild air just above a temperate water surface produces still another type of fog known as *arctic sea smoke*. It is common during the fall and early winter when cold air outbreaks from polar regions rush across the still mild waters of the Great Lakes. Visible proof of increasing amounts of moisture in the air, these fogs are the forerunners of heavy snows or rain showers on the downwind shores of these bodies of water (Figure 3-5). This "lake effect" precipitation and cloudiness is described in more detail in Chapter 6.

Like arctic sea smoke, contrails (trails of condensed vapor) form in the wake of jet aircraft when cold air is mixed with the warm, humid products of fuel combustion, but the majority of clouds above ground level are formed by the cooling of air to its dew point at a particular altitude. Vertical motion in the atmosphere produces the cooling because rising air is subject to decompression. Decompression lets air expand as it ascends to levels of lower pressure, causing cooling just as the spray from an aerosol can is cooled when

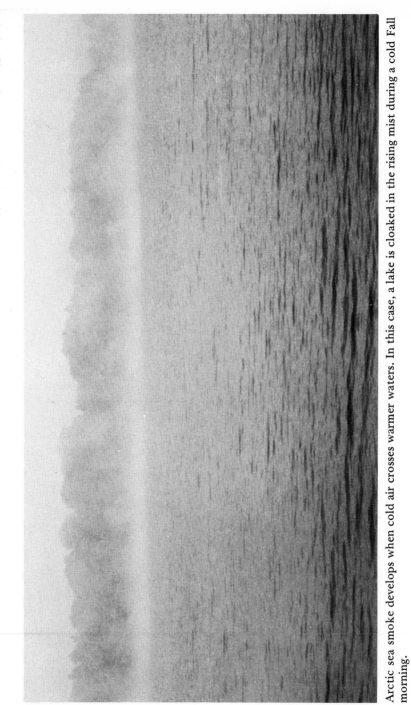

Arctic sea smoke develops when cold air crosses warmer waters. In this case, a lake is cloaked in the rising mist during a cold Fall morning.

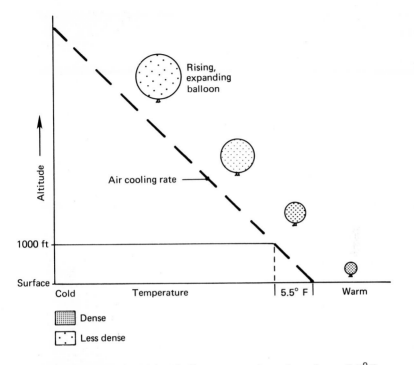

Figure 3-6 Air in the rising balloon expands and cools at 5.5°F per 1,000 feet. If the actual temperature of the air followed the dotted line, the balloon's contents would always be warmer so ascension would continue.

the pressurized product is released to room air of lower pressure.

The lifting can be induced by air flowing over a mountain or weather front, or where air converges and ascends. An area of lifting can also develop where the sun heats both land and adjacent air, producing the rising convection currents called *thermals*. Glider pilots know how to read the signs of rising air, and often use these currents to stay aloft. However, when the rising air is moist, thunderstorms develop in these currents. Such air mass thunderstorms randomly occur throughout the country during summer, especially in the Southeast.

When air is dry or unsaturated, the cooling rate is 5.5°F for each 1,000 feet of ascension. As in a hot air balloon, if the

Clouds that develop vertical, spired appendages reveal atmospheric instability.

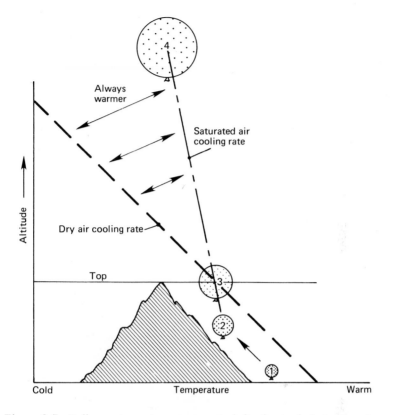

Figure 3-7 Balloon at any temperature to left of actual air temperature (dotted line) would not rise. If forced up a mountain or lifted in a thunderstorm (steps 1 and 2), it would cool at dry air rate. If saturation occurred at 2, the new cooling rate for saturated air would hold. As air was pushed to altitude of mountain top, it would cool at this slower rate, making it warmer than surroundings at point 3. From here, it would continue to ascend on its own.

temperature of an air parcel (in spite of this cooling) remains warmer than its surroundings, the air continues to rise. This is because the warmer air of the balloon or parcel is less dense (lighter) than the surrounding air it passes through (Figure 3-6). The atmosphere is termed "unstable" when this occurs, and the most visible manifestation of instability is the towering cloud associated with a thunderstorm's ascending air currents.

Sun warmed land and/or mountainous terrain are causing vertical motion, cooling of humid air and cloud formation above this Caribbean island. Ancient mariners used these cloud caps to navigate to unseen islands over the horizon.

Also at work in the cumulonibus cloud of a thunderhead is another process which keeps the rising air warmer than its surroundings — the release of latent heat from condensing water vapor. When moist air rises, it cools at the 5.5° rate until saturation (100 percent relative humidity). Thereafter, the release of heat from condensation slows the cooling to approximately 3°F per 1,000 feet (Figure 3-7).

Puffy vertical clouds (cumulus or extreme cumulonimbus) exhibit atmospheric instability, while flat clouds (stratus) indicate a stable atmosphere. In this case, little temperature difference exists between surrounding air and an air parcel (or balloon), and there is no driving force for vertical motion.

Descending air, on the other hand, is compressed which produces heating of 5.5°F for each 1,000 feet of downward motion. Whether going up or down, the temperature of the air is changing and, as we have noted, the relative humidity is changing, too.

Descending, warming air gives us cloudless skies because as the air warms without adding moisture, the relative humidity decreases below saturation. Ascending, cooling air, however, approaches saturation or 100 percent RH.

It is evident that clouds tend to form as air rises over a mountain, a front, or a heated section of the earth's surface. Once a cloud is generated, further vertical motion depends on the stability of the surrounding air. Thicker, precipitating clouds are the result of continued ascent and other factors; thinner, nonprecipitating clouds are found where this vertical motion is inhibited after condensation has taken place.

Remember that high pressure areas are characterized by sinking air, and highs inhibit clouds and precipitation; but low pressure areas are characterized by air masses rising over large areas, and tend to produce stormy weather. These lows cause most of the precipitation and cloudiness across the United States; in fact, one of them came to be known as the Great Blizzard of 1978.

4

LOWS

The cold winds on the back side of the Great Blizzard of 1978 were typical signs of a storm which has reached adulthood. At birth, those winds were light and from the northeast — the polar easterlies in our global surface model — and the light airs of the south were coriolis curving to the northeast, creating the prevailing westerlies.

The zone between conflicting airflows is called a *front* (Figure 4-1a). Suddenly, the front encounters a catalyst. It may be a mountain range or other topographical effect, or a local temperature irregularity, cold or warm body of water, or a trough aloft (Figure 4-1b). A bulge of lighter, warm air rises over the front, above the cooler air. Rising warm air defines low pressure. Other air rushes in to fill its place. The inrushing air coriolis curves to the right. The bulge or wave on the front soon develops into a counterclockwise eddy called a *cyclone* or *low pressure area* (Figure 4-1c).

40

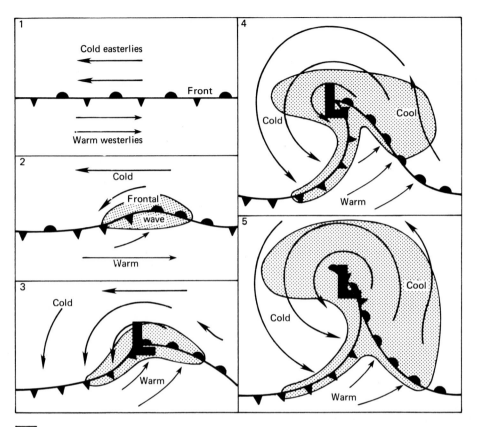

 Percipitation

Figure 4-1 The life cycle of a low pressure system. In the final stages, the system occludes which means cold air encircles the low, cutting energy supply.

Its diameter expands to hundreds of miles. On its east side, warm air is flowing northward, rising above the cooler, more dense air. This is a *warm front*. On its west side, cold air is ploughing into the warm air, creating a cold front. (Figure 4-1d). As it matures, the low draws in air from more distant latitudes. Cold winds howl from the far north while warm and increasingly humid air from the tropics rushes northward. Across the system, an imbalance exists between cold, dense air and warm, less dense air. This density discontinuity represents potential energy which is converted to kinetic energy, energy in motion which drives the storm. The circu-

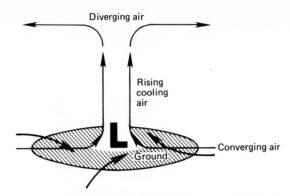

Figure 4-2 Horizontal and vertical circulation in a low. Converging surface airflow ascends and cools producing inclement weather common to lows. As in a chimney, the flow diverges aloft.

lation spirals (converges) toward the center, the lure of the lower pressure drawing the winds inward where they rise upward (Figure 4-2).

Over rough terrain, excessive friction on the spiraling circulation retards the forward motion, resulting in an airflow that moves more directly to the center of the low. In contrast, smooth surfaces such as the sea promote an airflow that is more circular about the low. In either case converging surface air must have an outlet aloft where the flow diverges, as above a chimney.

The barometer, which measures atmospheric pressure, is the instrument that meteorologists and weather buffs use to track lows. Standard atmospheric pressure is approximately 15 pounds per square inch. Let's think of the barometer as a scale measuring either high or low pressure (heavy or light weight). If we set the scale to 15 pounds and a high approaches, the scale will go up. Likewise, it will fall with an approaching low. For convenience, think of lows and highs as movie favorites Laurel and Hardy. The first letter in each name is a convenient device. Laurel, the thin, tie-flapping gentleman, would cause the scale to fall; Hardy, the jocular heavy man, will cause it to rise. With the barometer, we can tell if a low or high is approaching — but from which direction? The circulation around a low or high is the key. "A wind from the south has rain in her mouth," as the saying

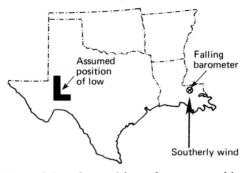

Figure 4-3 Determining the position of an approaching low pressure area

goes. For instance, if the wind is from the south and the barometer is falling, the low must be approaching from the west (Figure 4-3). If you stand with the wind at your back, the low would be to your left. In fact, if you stand with your back to the wind anywhere in the Northern Hemisphere, the low is always to your left.

In another example, if the wind is first from the southeast, then from the east and then from the northwest, and throughout the time the barometer fell and then rose, the low would have passed to the south of your position (Figure 4-4).

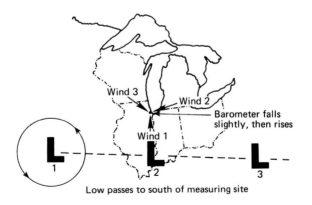

Figure 4-4 Shifting winds and barometric tendency give clues to positions of a low tracking nearby.

Table 4-1

WIND AND PRESSURE GUIDELINES   This chart summarizes decades of meteorological experience in the Northeast region. In this area winds from the west almost always bring high-pressure readings and good weather, while those from an easterly direction generally mean a falling barometer and rain or snow. A wind that swings from easterly to westerly usually brings with it a swift and welcome change — from bad weather to good.

Wind Direction	Barometer at sea level	Kind of weather to be expected
SW to NW	30.10 to 30.20 steady	Fair with little temperature change for one or two days
SW to NW	30.10 to 30.20, rising fast	Fair, followed by rain within two days
SW to NW	30.20 or above steady	Continued fair, with little temperature change
SW to NW	30.20 or above, falling slowly	Slowly rising temperature; fair for two days
S to SE	30.10 to 30.20, falling slowly	Rain within 24 hours
S to SE	30.10 to 30.20, falling fast	Wind rising in force; rain in 12 to 24 hours
SE to NE	30.10 to 30.20, falling slowly	Rain in 12 to 18 hours
SE to NE	30.10 to 30.20, falling fast	Rising wind; rain within 12 hours
E to NE	30.10 or above, falling slowly	In summer, light winds, rain not immediately likely; in winter, rain in 24 hours
E to NE	30.10 or above, falling fast	Rain probable in summer within 24 hours; in winter, rain or snow and windy
SE to NE	30.00 or below, falling slowly	Steady rain for one or two days
SE to NE	30.00 or below, falling fast	Rain and high wind, clearing within 36 hours
S to SW	30.00 or below, rising slowly	Clearing within a few hours, fair for several days
S to E	29.80 or below, falling fast	Severe storm imminent; clearing within 24 hours; colder in winter
E to N	29.80 or below, falling fast	Severe northeast gale, heavy rain; in winter, heavy snow and cold wave
GOING to W	29.80 or below, rising fast	Clearing and colder

Any combination of barometric pressure tendency and wind direction change can be analyzed to detect the movement of low or high pressure systems. It is most helpful for sailors on the high seas where there is little topographical interference with wind direction (Table 4-1).

In the northeast quadrant of the low pressure system, ascendency is most pronounced and nearer to the moisture source. This is where the warm and humid air is both rising in the chimney-like draft and overrunning the cooler air at the surface near and just to the north of the warm front. It is the sector of widespread precipitation and cloudiness. This is where the New England states were situated during the height of the Blizzard of 1978.

At the warm front, clouds ascend gradually. Near the front, low clouds may be attended by fog and drizzle. As if on a slanted table, they slope upward from this location as the mild, humid air moves uphill over the increasingly deep colder air below. Most precipitation occurs within the first 200 miles of this uplift (Figure 4-5).

Farther north (at the other end of the table) high, thin clouds are the first signs of moisture which has travelled upward along the sloping surface. Composed of tiny ice crystals at these high altitudes, these clouds sometimes give rise to halos about the sun or moon, popular subjects for weather forecasting lore.

> "Halo around the sun or moon
> rain or snow comes very soon"

On the back side, cold frontal clouds result from cold, dense air plowing into warm, humid air. This snowplow effect produces precipitation and cloudiness of shorter duration and greater intensity. Showers, thunderstorms, and gusty, rapidly shifting winds are trademarks (Figure 4-6).

After a cold front passes, moderate to strong winds blow from the northwest for a day or two before diminishing. In Texas they are called "blue northers." Locations subject to the northeast quadrant of passing low pressure systems are more likely to experience prolonged cloudy, damp, non-

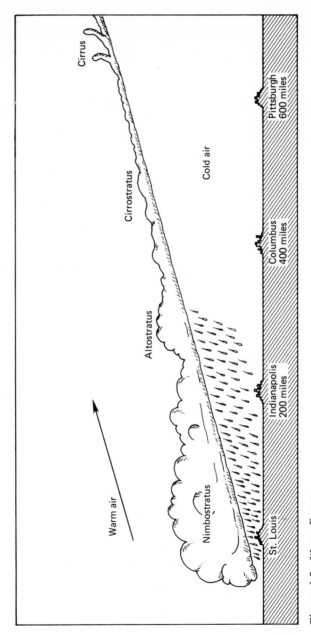

Figure 4-5   Warm Front

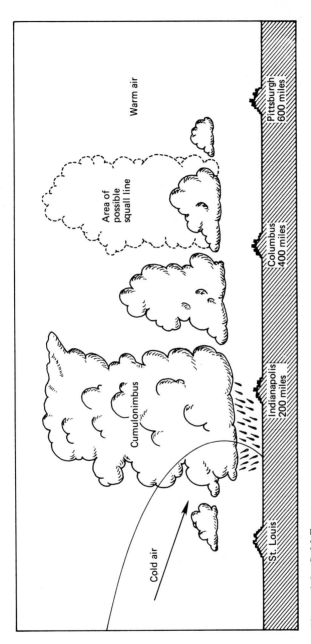

Figure 4-6 Cold Front

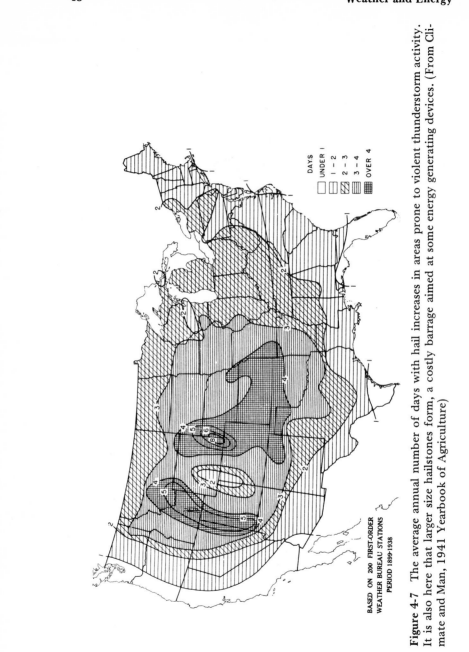

BASED ON 200 FIRST-ORDER
WEATHER BUREAU STATIONS
PERIOD 1899-1938

Figure 4-7 The average annual number of days with hail increases in areas prone to violent thunderstorm activity. It is also here that larger size hailstones form, a costly barrage aimed at some energy generating devices. (From Climate and Man, 1941 Yearbook of Agriculture)

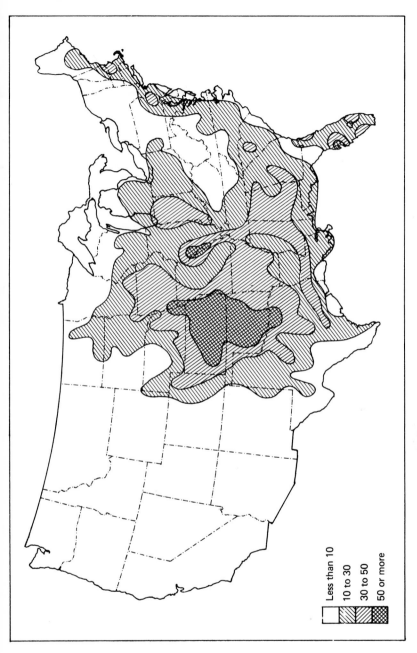

Figure 4-8 Tornado prone regions between 1916 and 1963.

Less than 10

10 to 30

30 to 50

50 or more

This developing thunderstorm may weigh millions of tons and pack enough energy to power a small city for a year. The cumulonimbus cloud may be singular as in an airmass thunderstorm, or numerous and in a solid, advancing line called a squall line.

violent weather. Areas frequented by cold frontal passages, in other words south of the tracking low, are more likely to experience weather of a shorter, more violent nature. Figures 4-7 and 4-8 show locations prone to these events.

It is here, in warm, moisture laden air, that thunderstorms reach severe levels and may be accompanied by strong, gusty winds, hail, lightning, and tornadoes. Each thunderstorm packs several million tons of water droplets which have supplied heat energy during condensation. Usually, the extreme weather precedes the cold front by 50 to 300 miles, in what is known as a *squall line*. Squall lines can grow to damaging proportions, particularly over flat terrain such as the Midwest and Great Plains. Typically, a squall line rips eastward accompanied by thunderstorms, strong winds, and possibly hail. Then a calm period ensues, followed by a second line of less intense showers or thunderstorms, accompanying the cold frontal passage. Lightning in any thunderstorm is dangerous — the chief weather killer that gets little publicity. The squall line is also a prime breeding ground for tornadoes. Tracing the development of squall lines, we are not surprised to find Tornado Alley, that part of the country which sees more than its share of tornadoes, in the same region as the more intense and numerous squall lines (Figure 4-8).

Tornadoes are small, powerful, rapidly moving storms which may leave little evidence of their presence just a few yards away; but where they do strike, complete devastation is likely.

Meteorologists cannot forecast tornadoes, nor can communication media always transmit a warning far enough in advance, so the public needs to be aware of tornado signs and must be able to act instantly. The obvious funnel cloud, excessive lightning, roaring noise, and very heavy rain are indicators to take action and not wait for the late arrival of a warning.

All of these hazardous weather occurrences threaten solar and wind collectors to varying degrees. Knowledge of how squall lines form and move can give you a headstart in preparing for violent winds of a squall line or the greenish

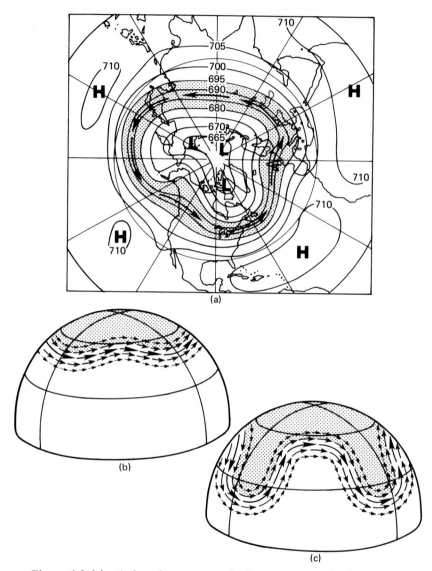

(a)

(b)

(c)

Figure 4-9 (a)   A three-loop pattern in the westerlies exhibiting moderate amplitude undulations. In this view from above the North Pole, the
snaking flow, called the circumpolar vortex, is driving cold air southeastward across Eastern Canada and Northeast US. Radical undulations
(c) are more common in Winter, supporting surface storminess as cold
air is driven southward on one side of the loop or trough and warmer
air is driven Northward on the other. Straighter West to East flow (b)
does not "support" surface lows and is characterized by fast moving,
less intense surface weather.

cloud often associated with thunderstorms containing hail. How do they move?

Like the eddy created by the oar of a boat, the spiraling low and fronts move downstream in the flow of a river; in this case a river of air above and to the sides of the eddy — the prevailing westerlies. Driven by the temperature contrast between poles and tropics, the higher altitude westerlies tend to be stronger, more active, and broader in scope during winter when temperature contrast is greatest. They recede northward in summer. Winter expansion also accompanies an increase in north-south undulations; these giant loops in the steering currents of air sweep southward, then northward, redistributing energy and driving cold air to Florida and tropical air to the North, causing the January thaws. The heart of this wind is known as the *jet stream*, which often attains speeds in excess of 100 miles per hour.

The looping westerlies snake around the top of the world making three, four, or five loops, but never a fraction thereof because the flowing snake's head must link up with the tail (Figure 4-9). Sometimes the undulations stall and drive temperature extremes north and south for prolonged periods. Rather than heralding a new ice or heat age, this simply means that part of the country is experiencing colder than normal weather, while another is sweltering in the return northward flow.

Caught up in this overlying flow, surface low pressure systems follow the trail and tend to intensify when the bottom of a loop (trough) nearly coincides with the surface system. At this time, the chimney-like convergence/divergence draft is at a maximum. The Blizzard of 1978 moved beneath a sharp trough which created an atmospheric whirlpool extending from surface to very high altitude (Figure 4-10). When this occurs storms slow, stall, vent their fury, and only then do they move eastward. In New England in February, 1978, this produced additional snow, strong winds, and high seas. These oddities are forecasting headaches because they can prolong storms, or cause a brief reversal in the normal west-to-east passage of weather systems. On *average*, however, storm tracks can be delineated (Figure 4-11).

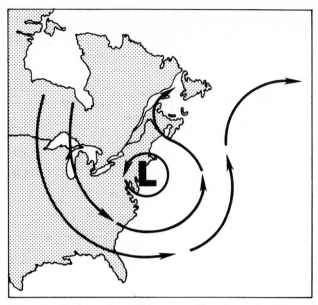

Figure 4-10   Radical looping of the westerlies above the Blizzard of '78 is called a cutoff low. Aircraft flying from Chicago to Florida did so in a strong tailwind, saving fuel and passenger time.

During winter, the tracks are farther south where strengthened polar air battles with the warmer air of the tropics. As the Northern Hemisphere is heated by the higher spring sun, these tracks recede to the north with the diminished polar air and shrinking westerlies. Excessive snow cover, countering surface heating through greater reflection of solar energy and increased nocturnal radiation, can delay the northward migration of the track. Premature snow cover can hasten the appearance of a southerly track earlier in the fall. Severe weather associated with cold fronts also migrates with the seasons; for example, Tornado Alley shifts northward during spring.

Warmer or colder ocean surface temperatures can affect the track. Since the seas warm and cool more slowly than the continents, a delay factor is evident. The most northerly tracks enter North America during late summer and early fall. High latitude Pacific waters are warmest at that time, not during the high sun of late June. This lag represents the slower response of the ocean to changes in solar intensity. Also note that surface water temperatures are nearly uniform

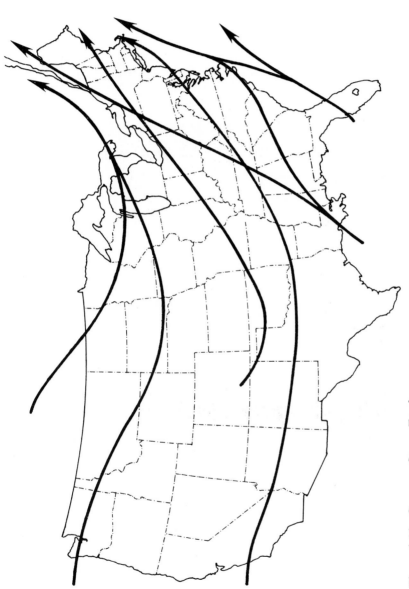

Figure 4-11   Common Storm Tracks

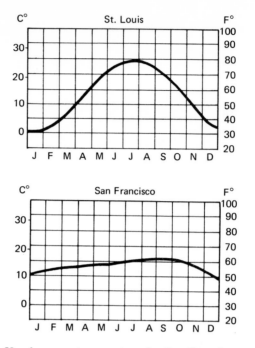

Figure 4-12 Yearly mean temperature for San Francisco and St. Louis. Both are at similar latitudes but exhibit sharply different temperature curves. The inland continental St. Louis location is subject to radical shifts because the land heats and cools more rapidly. San Francisco's marine environment reflects only small temperature changes similar to the minimal annual variations of ocean surface temperature.

throughout the seasons as opposed to the radical temperature variation of the land masses (Figure 4-12). During winter, cold air is entrenched farther south over the continents. Because of this, cold season lows exhibit a looping tendency; they enter North America at midpoint, sliding southeastward and then curving northeastward to exit into the Atlantic Ocean near or north of Cape Hatteras.

Whether entering North America via southern Alaska during summer or central California during the winter, low pressure systems have a limited lifetime as they progress eastward. After several days, the original system may disappear, or redevelop farther south or east. Or an aged, decaying system might spawn several new lows. In the lifetime diagram of a low pressure system, note that the sector of warm and humid air is being compressed during maturation (Figure 4-1). The cold front is overtaking the slower warm front because warm air can only erode its way northward along the warm front. The lighter warm air's impact is upward, over the colder surface air, and not straight ahead like the bulldozing cold, dense air.

Soon, only cold air will surround the low. The density discontinuity is lost, cutting off the energy supply. Lacking rising warm and humid air, the low also loses the energy from the heat of condensation. This is the death knell for a storm.

In summary, lows characterize the major atmospheric disturbances, storms. Up to a certain wind velocity, storms can provide practical energy. At high velocity, the winds are too powerful and become destructive. Practical energy is derived directly by conversion of the wind's kinetic energy into electricity or pumped water, and indirectly by its creation of ocean waves and currents, or by depositing water at higher elevations to be acted upon by gravity.

The temperature difference between poles and equator governs the strength of winds in the mid-latitudes: the greater this temperature difference, the stronger the winds. Lows are eddies in the atmospheric circulation patterns that help to transport the excess heat of equatorial regions toward the poles in order to decrease this temperature difference; since this is greater in winter, the most severe and persistent storms occur during that season.

In time, another low will come along. Between the lows a period of fair weather is likely. That is the domain of the anticyclone, the high pressure area.

5

HIGHS

Wednesday, February 8, 1978. A post-blizzard sun is warming the aching backs of snow shoveling New Englanders. A large high pressure area is moving into the region and several days of fair weather are ahead. This is the typical sequence on the back side of a departing low. At first, strong winds blow out of the northwest, causing the snow to drift. But they will diminish as the center of the high moves through. Then, they will become southerly and increase in speed, bringing warmer, more humid air northward as another low approaches. These wind shifts define the circulation around a high, in a clockwise or anticyclonic pattern (Figure 5-1).

As we saw earlier in the global circulation model, high pressure zones are found in a band at 30° and near the North Pole. Highs are regions of descending air which diverges or flows outward near the earth's surface. During descent, the air warms due to compression caused by the higher pressures at lower levels, similar to compression felt by descending divers at sea (Figure 5-2).

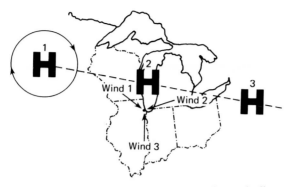

Figure 5-1 Shifting winds and barometric tendency indicate a high is tracking nearby. In this case, the barometer would rise until the high reached position 2, then fall.

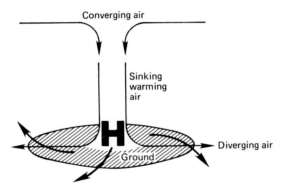

Figure 5-2 Horizontal and vertical circulation in a high. Sinking or subsiding air warms and is able to hold more moisture. If none is added, the air is "dried" accounting for the fair weather associated with high pressure.

The warming air can hold more moisture in the invisible water vapor state, but if no additional moisture is added, the result is to dry the air. This accounts for the fair weather regime of highs, the cold blue sky of the Arctic and the bright sun of Florida and the Southwest. Sinking air also produces a capping of the lower atmosphere called an *inversion*, an invisible shield which prevents vertical motion of near surface air to higher levels. Inversions are pronounced in the eastern semicircle of a high's circulation where sinking air is most prevalent.

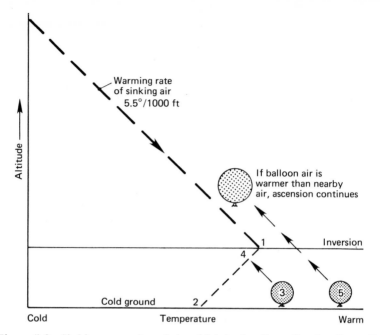

Figure 5-3 Sinking, warming air in a high is cloudless allowing for radiation of heat to space from near the earth's surface. This cooling extends upward to point 1, so actual temperature profile of air between surface and inversion is similar to 2-1. Rising hot air balloon 3 would cool at 5.5° per 1,000 feet until it got to point 4, where its temperature equals actual temperature of surrounding air, and stop. If air in balloon was warmed to higher temperature 5, ascension would continue beyond inversion.

Cold air accumulates near the earth's surface during clear nights, especially in winter, as heat radiates to space. At a depth of up to a few thousand feet, the cold air extends upward to meet with the descending, warming air at the inversion. The capping mechanism can be visualized by imagining a hot air balloon rising through the cooler, more dense air. The buoyed balloon, expanding and cooling, arrives at the inversion and suddenly encounters warmed air of similar density, or less. Since a difference no longer exists between balloon and outside air, the balloon stops rising. The hovering balloon would float like the warmed smoke from a chimney, which in winter rises, stops, and drifts horizontally, delineating the inversion.

Inversions can be bypassed if the rising air is warmer than that experienced at the inversion level. Daytime heating of surface air, if sufficient, will erase an inversion which may or may not reform the following night (Figure 5-3).

Inversions have important implications in air pollution because they trap pollutants in the lower atmosphere. Resultant turbid air diminishes solar intensity and solar collector efficiency. Colder air hovering near the earth and often associated with inversions, also routes any wind above its dominant dome and sometimes above the reach of wind generators. Diminishing winds at sunset reveal the detour; this diurnal effect is described in Chapter 8.

Descending airflow in a high diverges near the earth's surface, headed for lower pressure. Coriolis curving to the right, it exhibits the characteristic clockwise circulation (Figure 5-2). As in air escaping from an inflated tire, the difference between pressures in a high and a low determines speed of the air flow. This pressure gradient is most pronounced between well developed highs and lows (storms) and accounts for the strong, cold blast of wind following major storms (particularly in winter when polar or arctic highs are most pronounced).

During the Blizzard of 1978, strong winds also blew from the Canadian Maritimes westward across New England and then southward through New York State (Figure 5-4). The elongated circulation is due to a high that stretched from Hudson's Bay to Labrador. The high blocked progression of the storm through what would normally be an open northeast corridor; more importantly, it contributed to an airflow which travelled hundreds of miles across the ocean surface before crossing New England. Called *fetch*, this wind action over the water produced high seas and also humidified near-ocean air, adding to the extremely heavy snowfall total. Large high pressure areas interacting with storms are a prime feature of winter weather maps, but these arctic highs are only one part of a dual system.

The arctic highs are born of a long, dark winter's night, although highs of diminished strength prevail during the midnight sun of summer. In darkness, heat is radiated continu-

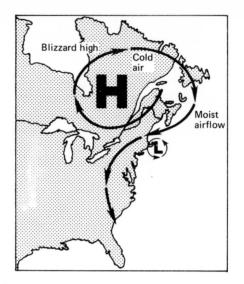

Figure 5-4 Blizzard high

ally to space and there is little, if any, heating from the absent or low level sun. Day after day, cold air builds to increasing depth, like a huge puddle atop the earth. Cold, dense air produces a high reading on barometers in spite of its relatively shallow depth, because its weight adds up rapidly. Greater depths of lighter warm air accomplish the same result at tropical locations (Figure 5-5). Extending to greater altitude, warm highs therefore are a deeper circulation feature than shallow cold highs.

As a result of extreme cold and no nearby moisture or heat source, the air which could not hold much moisture anyway is stable. Lack of moisture also enhances radiation of heat to space, reinforcing the cold regime. Strong inversions are also common.

Periodically, the cold air puddle spills southward; the polar front is the leading edge, followed by the polar easterlies. In more southerly latitudes, a storm may develop on the leading edge (see Chapter 4). These spillovers are most pronounced in winter and over land. Unlike oceans which warm and humidify from below, land helps maintain the cold, dry environment.

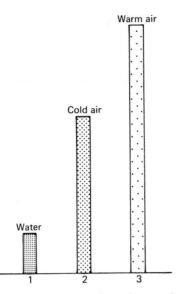

Figure 5-5 Weight or pressure experienced at points 1, 2, and 3 is equal. Density of material in each column determines its height.

The second high pressure system, found in a zone near 30° N latitude, is most pronounced over the ocean. Converging, sinking air from aloft warms and dries the underlying surface, producing sunny deserts on the east side of the circulation. As the flow progresses westward, added moisture and low level heating produces more numerous convection currents, which increases cloudiness and rainfall.

The western side of the Atlantic-dwelling Bermuda high is the warm, humid environment of the Southeast United States. Its eastern side is the African desert. Likewise, the deserts of the Southwest United States are situated on the eastern side of the Pacific high's circulation. Both Atlantic and Pacific highs are semi-permanent features of the southern oceans, and expand northward during warm season as the warmer air of greater depth produces high barometric readings farther north, and the westerlies recede toward the Pole. Dog-day heat and humidity then penetrate to Canada in the southerly flow around the Bermuda high (Figure 5-6). In the West, an enlarged Pacific high closes the door to storms, routing them far to the north and treating the Pacific Northwest to sunny weather.

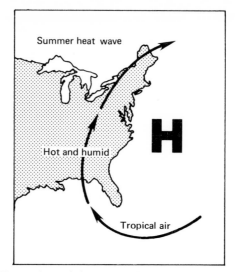

Figure 5-6   Expansion of the Bermuda high during summer oftentimes results in "heat waves" as tropical air circulates northward for a prolonged period.

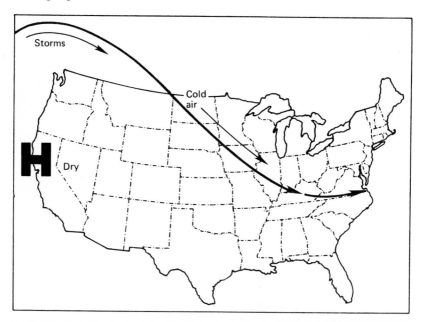

Figure 5-7   Summer expansion of the Pacific high blocks storms, routing them far to the north. This is the sunniest time of the year in the Pacific Northwest states. Sometimes, this pattern develops during winter and while the West Coast enjoys sunny, mild weather, the Midwest and East experience extremely cold weather.

Clear skies associated with the eastern side of the Pacific high drew population long before the sunbelt migration of today. Cliff dwelling Indians in the Southwest utilized passive solar heating and rock storage during winter and overhanging cliffs for shade during summer.

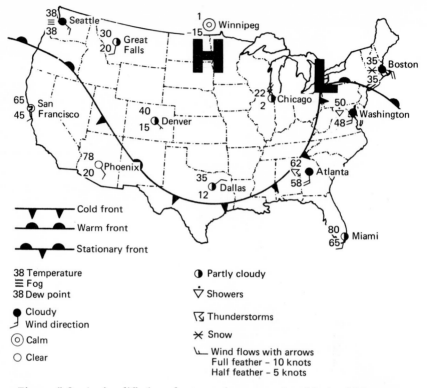

Cold front

Warm front

Stationary front

38 Temperature
≡ Fog
38 Dew point

● Cloudy
↲ Wind direction

◎ Calm

○ Clear

◑ Partly cloudy

∇̇ Showers

⩗ Thunderstorms

✕ Snow

∟ Wind flows with arrows
Full feather – 10 knots
Half feather – 5 knots

Figure 5-8 A simplified surface weather map. A cold, dry high pressure area is settling into the Midwest while a low is moving eastward attended by snow and rain as warmer and more humid air is drawn northward. Hundreds of weather reporting stations, such as those pictured here, facilitate analysis of current weather and projections of future weather. (See appendix).

In summary, shallow, cool continental highs spill southward from high latitudes, especially during winter; warm, deep oceanic highs migrate northward from the tropics, especially during summer. These motions are syncopated to the tune of lows passing between and around the high, drawing heat and humidity to divergent extremes of latitude. By following these continual shifts on weather maps, meteorologists can track and forecast weather from coast to coast (Figure 5-8).

Compared to the speedy lows the highs are heavyweights, lumbering north, south, east, and at times west. Periodically they stall and prolong fair weather at one location. In general they are characterized by light breezes, which implies that there is less energy available for wind power, and by less cloudiness in the sky, which implies more sunshine for direct solar energy processes. Sunnier and drier air in polar highs and on the eastern side of oceanic highs implies greater evaporation of moisture, so highs play an important part in the hydrological cycle of the earth's atmosphere.

With time, the air in the lower levels of the high tends to assume the characteristics of the surface below. We have already described the cold, dry arctic highs which reflect their birthplace as well as the warm and humid tropical highs associated with southern ocean areas. These characteristics fall into specific categories of air, called air masses.

6

AIR
MASSES

Cold, moist polar air contributed to the heavy snowfall during the Blizzard of 1978, and it was cold, dry polar air that swept New England after the storm. These pools of air, called air masses, usher in new regimes of weather which may or may not linger until another low approaches.

Air masses gather in two locations, the tropics and the poles. Tropical air, because of the vast oceanic expanse at lower latitudes, is predominantly humid. Polar air can be dry or moist, but holds little water compared to tropical air. Both begin to change as they leave their source region or spawning ground, where they acquired specific values of temperature and humidity. They are modified by the surface over which they travel and, with time, begin to lose identity.

Cold continental polar air, associated with a polar dwelling high pressure area, is stable air characterized by fair weather.

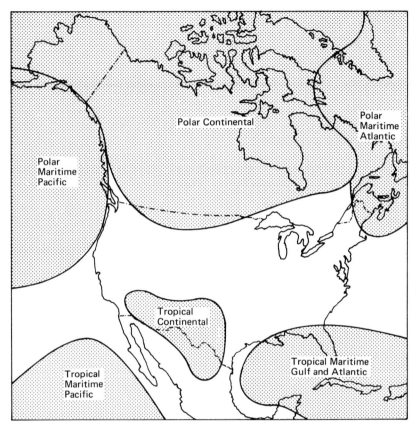

Figure 6-1 Air masses of North America and their source regions

In summer, this more temperate air mass brings refreshing relief from heat waves.

When spilling southward, continental polar air is modified in the lower levels by increased solar radiation heating the ground below. Ice-free lakes provide additional heat or moisture. Like the waviness you see above a radiator, currents of warm air (convection currents) rise through the air mass, carrying warmth and humidity skyward. Arctic sea smoke can be the first sign of this process. The once stable air develops a new wrinkle, a warmer, more humid base layer. Since warmer air will rise, the air mass tends to turn over and becomes agitated or unstable. Clouds form above the rising air and the once cloudless polar air now exhibits a low level

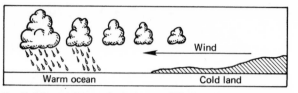

Figure 6-2 Cold continental air is modified and becomes cloudy as it crosses relatively mild ocean or lake waters. The lake or ocean effect ceases when waters freeze.

cloud deck. Increased instability means that the air will continue to rise, resulting in greater vertical developmemt of the clouds. Passage across the Great Lakes or other large bodies of water produces clouds that stretch skyward, cool, and release their moisture as snow or rain showers (Figure 6-2). Lake-effect precipitation is most intense where the cloud, driven by prevailing winds, moves onshore and runs into marked cooling.

Upper New York State and cities such as Buffalo and Rochester are particularly vulnerable to heavy lake-effect snows, since they are near the shores of Lakes Erie and Ontario where prevailing winter winds are from the northwest quadrant. Muskegon, Michigan, averages 87 inches of snow per year; directly across the lake, Milwaukee receives only 43 inches.

Ocean-effect snow also occurs when cold air crosses New England, becomes unstable over the adjacent warmer ocean waters, and dumps snow on Cape Cod. Occasionally, the entire ocean area just off the East Coast experiences ocean-effect cloudiness and precipitation. The clouds delineate a near perfect shadow of the shoreline as dry air leaves the continent and becomes cloud-decked some 50 miles at sea.

Solar collection capability can be affected adversely in areas downwind of large bodies of water and subjected to cold prevailing winds crossing the water. In particular, much of Michigan, northern Indiana, Ohio, and Pennsylvania, as well as Upper New York State, experiences this limitation. It is important to note that during warm seasons, these locations

As a storm churns offshore, cold, continental air moves southeastward and becomes cloudy in a near perfect shadow of the U.S. coastline. Increased snowcover and cloudiness can also be seen downwind of the Great Lakes.

experience more sunshine than surrounding areas, due to the stabilizing colder air from the water.

Maritime polar air, having its source region or birthplace over the sparse, unfrozen northern seas, is cloud-decked much of the time. During the cold season it is radically cooled to condensation just above the ocean surface. The most common source region is the North Pacific; from where this air mass rolls onto the West Coast. Rising and cooling as it crosses

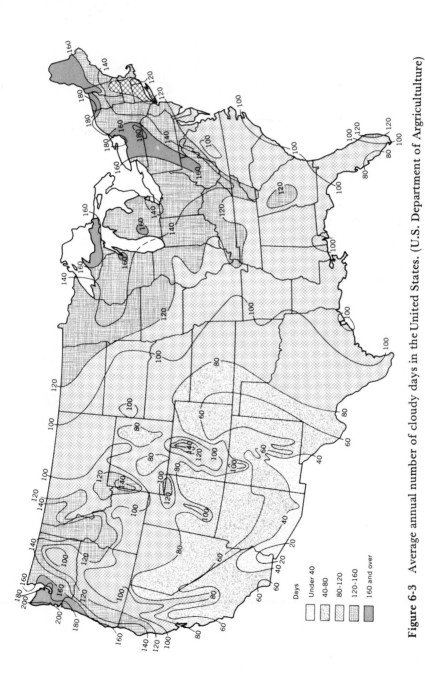

Figure 6-3 Average annual number of cloudy days in the United States. (U.S. Department of Argricultulture)

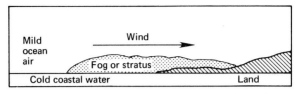

Figure 6-4 Fog or low cloudiness results when air is cooled to its dew-point by cold ocean waters along the West Coast.

the coastal mountains, it drops snow and rain on the windward slopes. The skier's delight, however, can be the solar collector's lament. Prolonged cloudiness as experienced in Northern California, Oregon, and Washington signals its presence (Figure 6-3). Travelling inland, maritime polar air also stagnates in the Great Basins of the West. Further cooling over the land results in prolonged valley fogs in places like California's San Joacquin Valley or the Great Salt Lake desert.

During summer, maritime polar air is stable; that is, cool in the lower levels. But it is warmer than the cold ocean currents off the California coast (Figure 6-4). Further cooling of the lower level as it crosses these waters produces a relative increase in humidity and condensation, resulting in widespread fog or low clouds. This weather penetrates inland in a cyclic manner depending on solar input. Maximum solar heating inland generates convection currents which leave a void as the air rises. Coastal air rushing inland to fill that void carries the fog or low clouds with it. The movement is most pronounced through breaks in coastal mountain ranges, such as at San Francisco Bay. At first, the arriving moist air is mostly dried by the inland heat, and the fog evaporates; gradually, though, the cool, foggy air prevails. Then the warm convection currents are cut off, eliminating the driving mechanism, and the inclement weather retreats to the coast. But once the sun gets back to work, another driving force is established and the cycle is reestablished.

A typical daily cycle in the Bay area goes like this: solar heating draws fog and low clouds inland to reside for the night. The murky weather burns off in the morning as the rising sun heats and dries the air, but then convection currents develop and lure the dismal weather back for an afternoon encore (Figure 6-5).

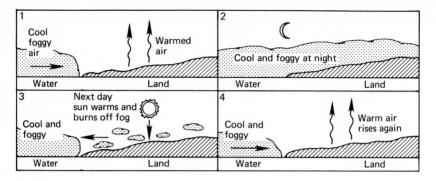

Figure 6-5 A typical sun and fog cycle in California results from alternate heating and cooling of the land.

Moist polar air makes an occasional appearance in the Northeast United States, too. The air mass settles southward with a high pressure area in the vicinity of the Canadian Maritimes. When this happens, mild weather from Maine to New York can be interrupted suddenly by a wind shift to the east and attendant low clouds, drizzle, fog, and cool temperatures. This "backdoor" cold front, named because it travels in an opposite direction from what one might expect, may linger for several days and then retreat out to sea (Figure 6-6).

In its place, one might expect a return of fair, mild continental air which originated as hot, dry air far to the south in a small region of the Southwestern United States. It rarely appears in winter. Continental tropical air is cloudless in spite of the warm vertical currents established by insolation, because it is extremely dry. As it travels north and east, additional moisture is added to the lower levels, causing an increase in cloudiness. In time, additional moisture causes this air mass to become indistinct from maritime tropical.

The dominant summer air mass over much of the United States — maritime tropical — is associated with the Bermuda high pressure area that lingers in the vicinity of its namesake. Oppressive heat and humidity circulates from the Gulf of Mexico to Canada. Each afternoon, maximum solar heating produces convection currents which lift the warm, moist air to great heights. Showers and thunderstorms develop within the rising columns of air, and then dissipate. The sun then re-

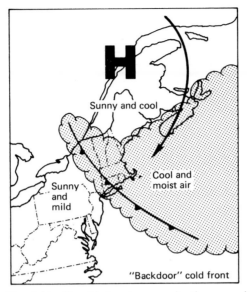

Figure 6-6 A "backdoor" cold front moves in the opposite direction of most weather systems.

appears and the process repeats. Note this thermostat-like control, not found in continental air. Each time there is increased solar input, convection currents produce clouds or showers which shield the sun. The convection ends, the cloud or shower dissipates, and again the sun sets to work.

Maritime tropical air is by far the chief moisture supplier for the United States during winter. Its northerly ventures in the eastern half of the country fuel the heavy snowstorms in Chicago and the "Nor'easters" of New England. In the West, lows moving in from the Pacific carry this air mass to a watery collision with the coastal mountains and copious winter rains that seem to slide California into the sea.

The perspective of weather across the United States, as we have seen, is a changing pattern of lows, fronts, highs, and attendant air masses that continually interact to produce the various types of weather. In examining these phenomena, several basic principles have become evident. A review of these principles will help you to understand most, if not all, weather producing events. A weather prophecy primer follows:

1. Warm or moist air is less dense, or lighter, and tends to rise; cold air is more dense, or heavier, and tends to sink.

2. Heavier air creates high pressure — Olivier Hardy; lighter air creates low pressure — Stan Laurel.

3. Just as water seeks its own level, high pressure air seeks to equalize with low pressure, resulting in airflow between the two.

4. Rising dry air cools and descending dry air warms at about 5.5°F per 1,000 feet.

5. Warm air can hold more water vapor than cold air. Cooling of moist air will cause the relative humidity to increase until the air is saturated. The rate of change approximates a doubling of relative humidity for each 18°F temperature fall. Conversely, heating of cold, saturated air will cause relative humidity to decrease, since the warmer air will be able to hold more moisture. This rate of change approximates a halving of relative humidity for each 18°F temperature rise.

Utilizing several of these principles, we can discover how an air mass changes its identity as it passes over a specific location.

Most of these changes are easily seen when we view maritime tropical air invading the West Coast. Wind blowing perpendicular to the mountains is forced upward, cooling the air and increasing its relative humidity. At saturation, clouds form and finally precipitaion develops. Clouds and precipitaion formed in this manner are called *orographic*. The more moist and inbound the mass, the more readily clouds and precipitation will develop lower on the mountainside. Rolling over the top and descending, the air is compressed, resulting in warm, dry air as in the subsiding air in a high pressure area. A closer look reveals that this passage has changed the complexion of the original air mass. During ascendency, moisture content is diminished by rain or snowfall. But condensation has also liberated heat originally used to evaporate moisture into the air as water vapor. As a result, cooling is not as rapid as 5.5°F per 1,000 feet. The slower cooling rate continues with condensation until the air ceases to rise at the top of the mountain. But on the other side in dry air, greater heating due to compression occurs; therefore, a look at the air at an

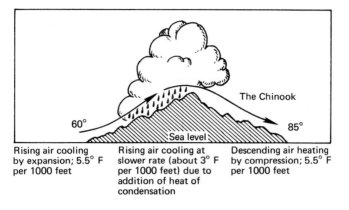

Figure 6-7 Weather and airmass changes incurred when airflow traverses mountains.

equal level on either side of the mountain reveals warmer and drier air on the descending side (Figure 6-7). Primarily for this reason, Death Valley is the hottest and driest location in the United States. These warm, dry, downslope winds called chinooks can also bring sudden sunny and warm weather to otherwise chilled locations in Montana, Wyoming, and Colorado.

Airflows over smaller mountains produce less extreme results, but it is obvious which side of a mountain is more favorable for location of solar collectors. This decision must be made with the prevailing wind direction in mind, since the mountain range orientation and windflow perpendicular to the range are prerequisites.

Downslope warming is also part of the reason why Boston, for instance, is slightly warmer and periodically drier than other areas at similar latitudes just a few hundred miles west.

Experiencing less precipitation, river basins situated downwind of mountains see diminished flows while those on the upwind side show more potential for hydroelectric power development. The Big Thomson Canyon system in Colorado tries to equalize this deficiency on the eastern slopes of the Rockies by transporting water from water-rich upwind slopes to shaded terrain (see Chapter 9).

Let's recap: Air masses are distinct traveling bodies of atmospheric energy with the potential to create some form of disturbance in which their energy will be liberated. Their energy content in the form of water's latent heat of vaporization and sensible heat (heat ascribed to their temperature) can be liberated by interaction with other air masses, with land, and with the oceans. We have already seen one of the extreme possibilities in the Blizzard of 1978.

Other considerations involving localized weather can have significant effect on energy collection and storage. The chapters which follow are devoted to these concerns.

7

SOLAR
ENERGY

During each 24-hour day the earth receives ten quintillion
Btu of energy from the sun; this is ten million million million
Btu, or some 20,000 times the energy used by all of humanity
in the same period of time! It receives this energy quite
regularly, as it has for approximately 5 billion years, and
probably will for another 5 billion years before the sun
enters its projected red giant phase, expands, and consumes
the earth.

The sun's bountiful flow of energy to a point on the earth's
surface really is not continuous. Intensity of ground level
solar radiation, called *insolation*, varies. It is subject to several
kinds of variation and interruption, the most obvious of
which is the diurnal cycle, the 24-hour day-night period.
Cloudy weather also affects insolation, and seasonal variations cause changes in the angle of the incoming rays. And
finally, it appears that the intensity of the sun's output itself
may be subject to some variation over longer or shorter
periods.

The harvests of fall in the Northern Hemisphere mark a declining sun, but not necessarily a weaker one. In fact, during winter the earth is about 3.1 million miles closer to the sun and 7 percent more energy is available than in June. The earth's tilt is what causes the Northern Hemisphere to shy away from solar radiation in winter. Of course, this shortens the duration of the day and spreads incoming rays over a larger surface area, diminishing their intensity (see Chapter 2). Since the solar beam also must travel through more atmosphere, additional losses occur through scattering and absorption. Of what does this bountiful flow of energy consist, and what part does weather play in the interruption of a steady flow of solar energy?

Inside the sun at various levels, somewhat like the layers of an onion, a complicated series of nuclear and chemical reactions is going on. Near the center, where temperatures reach millions of degrees, nuclear fusion reactions liberate the energy that is the source of the energy the earth ultimately gets from the sun. We cannot reproduce this particular kind of nuclear fusion energy on earth yet, because we haven't figured out how to keep the nuclear reactants continuously in touch with each other. The sun's gravity, however, is strong enough to solve this problem, so the reacting particles don't get blown away from each other by the liberated energy as they do in a hydrogen bomb, another example of nuclear fusion. The energy liberated in the nuclear fusion processes then works its way out through the various layers, each of which produces different reactions, until at the diffuse gaseous "surface" of the sun energy is emitted at the rate of 3,300 million million million million Btu per second, roughly a billion times more energy in a *second* than all the people in the world use in a decade.

This energy shoots out in all directions around the sun into what is essentially empty space, except for the planets and their satellites. The portion that reaches the earth is almost entirely pure energy in the form of electromagnetic radiation. This radiation consists of small packages (quanta) of energy having no mass, each characterized by electromagnetic vibrations of a certain wavelength.

The sun's energy arrives at the earth after an eight-minute trip through space in the form of this electromagnetic radia-

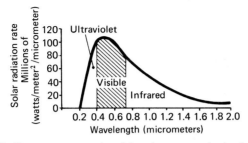

Figure 7-1 Radiant energy emitted by the sun peaks in the visible portion of the various wavelengths which comprise the spectrum.

tion. "Sunshine" is a better word in many ways, but it leaves the impression that the energy is all visible light (Figure 7-1). Actually, about half the sun's energy received at the earth's surface is visible; the other half is the infrared radiation that can be felt coming from a hot radiator. A small amount is in the ultraviolet spectrum, wavelengths shorter than that of light. Although its effects can be pronounced (ultraviolet causes sunburn, suntan, and skin cancer), the amount of energy in this spectral region is only a small fraction of the total in sunshine.

Within the visible part of the spectrum, our eyes see the different wavelengths as different colors. The shortest wavelength we can see, a bit less than 0.4 microns, is violet; as the wavelength increases we see blue, green, yellow, orange, and red until, at a bit beyond 0.7 microns, the wavelength is too long for our eyes to see as light. Then our skin takes over as receptor, allowing us to "see" the radiation as heat.

This form of energy used for practical purposes is distinctly different from that contained in more traditional sources of energy. Coal, oil, and natural gas, for example, usually are burned to release chemical energy in the form of heat. The sun's radiant energy, however, is absorbed on a dark colored surface or in a dark liquid to produce heat, or it is absorbed by certain solid state devices to produce electricity directly.

The spectrum of wavelengths received by the earth from the sun is shown in Figure 7-2, where the height of the graph at

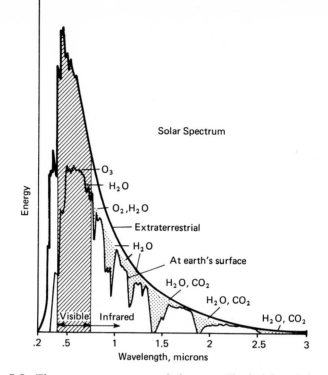

Figure 7-2 The energy spectrum of the sun. The height of the graph indicates the amount of energy in sunshine at the corresponding wavelength. The upper line is the spectrum at the top of the earth's atmosphere, and the lower line shows what gets through to the surface of the earth after absorption by gaseous constituents in the atmosphere.

a given wavelength indicates how much of the sun's energy is characterized by that wavelength. The wavelength scale is given in microns, or millionths of a meter, so that part of the sun's spectrum visible in a rainbow is represented by wavelengths between about 0.4 and 0.7 microns. Wavelengths shorter than this are ultraviolet radiation, and longer wavelengths are the infrared radiation which we feel as heat but do not see as color.

The upper line in Figure 7-2 shows the sun's spectrum at the top of the earth's atmosphere. But in passing through the air, some wavelengths are absorbed by ozone, carbon dioxide, water vapor, and a small amount by nitrogen, so that at the earth's surface the spectrum looks like the lower line in the figure; not much energy in the ultraviolet, about half in the visible, and half in the infrared to about 2.5 microns, beyond which there is no significant sunshine.

All warm bodies emit this kind of radiation, with roughly the same general enveloping shape to the spectral curve, but the curve moves to longer wavelengths as the temperature of the body decreases. Not many objects on earth are as hot as the sun (11,000°F), so very little of the radiation they emit is in the visible wavelength region. Molten steel is one example of a material warm enough to shine in the visible, but most other warm bodies shine only in the infrared, like the ashes of an extinquished fire. Objects at room temperature or the temperature of a radiator, for example, shine mostly at wavelengths longer than ten microns, far from wavelengths that characterize sunshine.

This immediately suggests a useful way to capture the sun's energy to heat homes and to provide hot water. If we can make a container out of a material that is transparent to sunshine but opaque to longer wavelengths (warmshine?), then the sunshine will enter and be absorbed by some object inside which becomes heated, but the radiation emitted by the heated body won't be able to shine out. Since the "window" is opaque at these wavelengths, it will absorb the long wavelength radiation, become heated, and then reradiate this absorbed energy in two directions — roughly half toward the outside and the other half back into the container (Figure 7-3). We now have a device which likes to receive and absorb sunshine, but is reluctant to let it escape, and we can think of how to use the absorbed energy for some practical purpose, like heating a room or a liquid which can later be tapped for its heat.

This is the idea behind many solar collectors on the market today. Glass and some plastics have almost exactly the characteristics described above for the "window" that passes radiant energy preferentially in one direction. Glass is highly transparent in the sunshine wavelength region out to three microns, and opaque at longer wavelengths. Sometimes this is called the "greenhouse effect," although it is not a particularly well chosen name. Greenhouses operate more by keeping cold winds out than by preventing radiation heat loss, although radiation is part of the story.

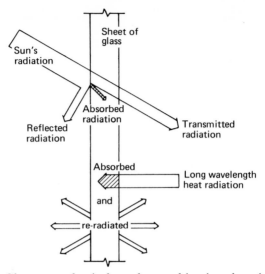

Figure 7-3 Glass acts selectively to let sunshine in, where it can be absorbed. The long wavelength (infrared) radiation emitted by the absorber inside, however, is absorbed by the glass and partly re-radiated back into the enclosed space.

The earth's atmosphere itself creates a kind of greenhouse effect. Carbon dioxide, present in the atmosphere to the extent of about .03 percent, and water vapor both have optical properties analogous to those of glass; sunshine gets through, but "earthshine" is partly absorbed as it tries to get out. Changing the atmospheric content of carbon dioxide, therefore, as we do by burning fossil fuels, could have a long-term tendency to change the earth's mean temperature, and consequently the climate. Climatologists are concerned that as worldwide energy use increases, the widespread burning of fossil fuels may change the climate in this way.

Still another, quite different method of using the sun's radiation to produce energy is the *photovoltaic* effect. When sunshine strikes the surface of certain properly prepared semiconductors, electricity is produced directly without the need for mechanical or thermal processes of any kind. Silicon wafers commonly are used to make photovoltaic electricity and, from the 1950s when the cost of electricity produced this way was more than $1,000 per watt in full sunlight, the

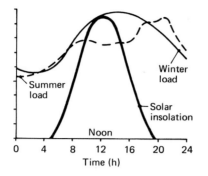

Figure 7-4 Hourly variations in insolation, and winter and summer demands for electricity.

cost has come down to roughly $5 per watt, with every prospect for further cost reductions in the near future.

Even at the present cost, photovoltaic electricity competes with electricity required in remote locations or in some foreign nations that do not have an extensive electrical distribution network in place.

If the earth were everywhere equally sunny, there would be little more for us to say on solar energy, but of course it isn't. Weather also plays an important part in any strategy to use the sun's energy in a practical way.

The practical aspects of solar heating are less familiar today than those of the oil, gas, or coal furnace, so techniques for sizing solar equipment to meet a home heating requirement are also less familiar. Furthermore, sizing solar systems tends to be a bit more complex, since orientation of the solar receiving surface plays an important part in the system's performance.

Also, in order to predict the performance of a solar heating system in somebody's house, you have to know how much sunshine the location receives, and how much heat or electricity the system will be expected to deliver (Figure 7-4). So the variability of the sunshine and of the outdoor temperature both affect the prediction.

One way to assess the likely performance of a solar heating system is to construct a mathematical model of each of its components, and then to calculate, using weather data in the simulation, the performance hour by hour over a period of time. Several computer simulations already formulated are available to architects and engineers for use in designing solar heating systems. Obviously knowledge of the weather and its variability in a given location is important to such a simulation, and fortunately many locations in the United States keep careful weather records.

Even with a large computer the calculations are lengthy, especially if you are interested in performance over an entire year. Furthermore, how can you be sure that a year chosen at random is "typical" of the location?

Monthly average figures for sunshine could be misleading, for example, although they are commonly used. Imagine a month that consists of 15 sunny days followed by 15 cloudy days, and another that consists of 30 partly sunny days with the same average sunshine as the first month. Because of the relatively short heat storage time in a solar heating system, the second month will predict better performance than the first, though the monthly average sunshine is the same. So the question of what constitutes "typical" weather is a good one, even if weather records are available over a long period.

One way the question has been resolved is by having the computer examine weather records over a long period, and then construct a shorter period of time — a week, say — that represents a month. The "typical week" must have the same average intensity of sunhine and the same average outdoor temperature as the longer period it represents and the sequence of sunny, partly sunny, and cloudy days also must be the same as the most probable sequence over the longer period. In this way a "typical week" in March can be made to represent thirty years of Marches if the weather records are available. Using this abbreviated weather in the simulation can save a great deal of computer time and expense as well as ensuring that we haven't chosen an unusual weather period.

The possibility that weather correlations might help make solar energy more effective has intrigued scientists in the field in recent years. For example, it is easy to prove a strong correlation between the days of intense sunshine in the summer and those requiring air conditioning of buildings, especially in the Southwest. Therefore, solar assisted air conditioning systems have a natural correlation going for them, so long-term storage of solar energy for this purpose is less important.

A possible correlation between a requirement for heat in the winter and days of bright sunshine is less obvious, though from our study of weather phenomena we can see that it is at least possible. Consider those days immediately following passage of a cold front followed by dry, arctic air. Heated to indoor temperatures, the air is exceedingly dry, and rapid evaporation from the skin gives you a chill. Strong winds after lows and fronts pass steal heat from a house, and drafts produce an additional chill. Finally, the clear, dry air permits maximum radiational cooling of the earth's surface at night. With the already frigid arctic air, these periods are the coldest of the winter.

The air's clarity also makes these the sunniest times as well. So we could expect that this sunshine-cold correlation works for solar energy to provide winter heat, just as the sunshine-hot correlation works in summer. The relationship is not valid where cold air crosses water and rapidly clouds up. However, the negative effects are not as drastic as you might suppose, since the cold air in crossing water, warming, and clouding up brings warmer nighttime temperatures to the area, thus diminishing heating requirements.

Another correlation involving clouds reveals that loss of solar collection in a cloudy, warm frontal zone is offset by the warmer air advancing on the area as well as the lessening to almost nothing of nighttime radiational cooling.

Relating other weather fluctuations across the United States and solar availability, Dr. Walter Hoecker of Air Resources Laboratories has charted the relative potential of solar heating in various regions (Figure 7-5). Using solar energy incident on a tilted surface (latitude plus $10°$) and heating requirements of a standard building, Hoecker has produced a map that generally delineates regions of effective solar heat-

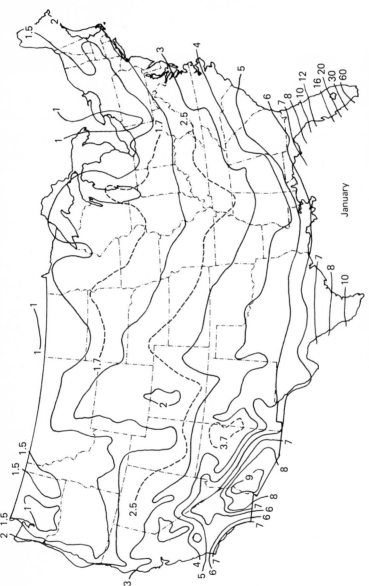

Figure 7-5 January solar radiation compared to heating demand in the United States. Isolines indicate relative effectiveness of solar energy in meeting heating demand when compared to a base where least effective. The eastern Great Lakes states experience much cloudiness and cold weather and are therefore assigned the value of 1.

ing efficiency in January. Scarcity of data compels caution in strict interpretation of boundaries.

The map assigns the value 1 to a base zone in the eastern Great Lakes which experiences high heating demand and low solar availability. This zone includes Buffalo, New York where tilted solar collectors would supply the lowest portion of heating demand. Relative to the base, St. Louis, Missouri, solar collectors would supply twice the required heating and Miami's collectors would gather an excessive 60 times the required heating demand. Applying percentages to these figures allows for interregional comparison. For instance, tilted solar collectors that supplied 20 percent of a building's heating needs in Buffalo would supply 40 percent for the same building in St. Louis and 1,200 percent in Miami. The excess could be used for cooling or dehumidification in southern latitudes.

The higher efficiency of solar heating in the lee of the Rockies is but one of the correlations already discussed in Chapter 6. Downslope winds (chinooks) clear and warm the air, enabling solar heating to be more efficient.

Defined by the Greeks, the term *climate* reflected the importance of the sun in determining various types of weather indigenous to an area. It turns out that they were not far off track, because as we have seen, solar input is at the heart of the weather machine. In addition, the seas and landmasses combine with insolation to produce a variety of weather patterns, the sum of which is *climate*.

Climatological values are available only where long-term measurement of daily weather is practiced. Knowledge of meteorology is helpful in interpolating for a location between two measuring points, because various parameters may vary radically due to influences of terrain or water.

The climate of Boston, for example, can be deduced from observations gathered in the immediate city; but a few miles inland, away from urban and water influence, the climate is very different. Sparsely populated areas, having little recorded weather history and widely spaced measuring points on variable terrain, are difficult to interpolate. In this case,

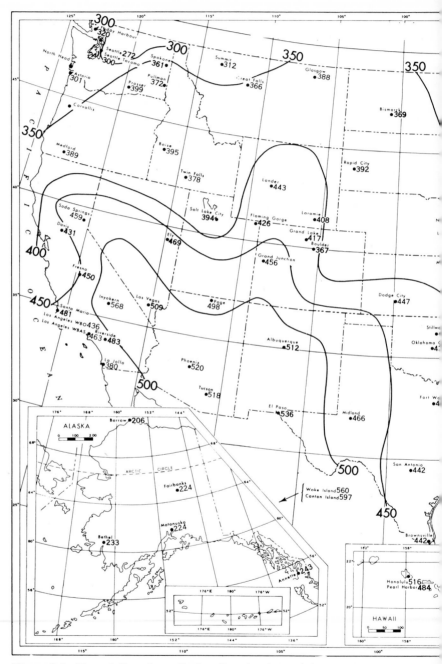

Figure 7-6   Mean daily solar radiation (Langleys), annual.

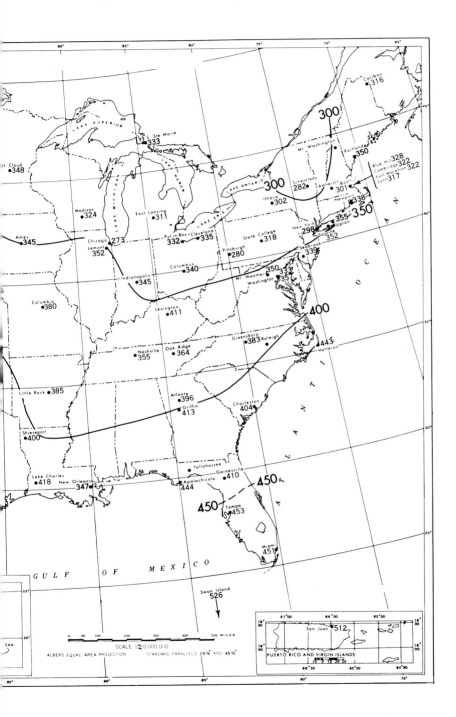

direct measurement and recordkeeping seems to be the only solution.

The solar radiation recorded in the *Climatic Atlas of the United States* accounts for average cloudiness and atmospheric turbidity (Figure 7-6). The numbers represent amount of direct beam and diffuse insolation on a horizontal surface. It is obvious that collectors tilted so that their surface is perpendicular to the incoming radiation will receive more of both direct and reflected radiation where surface reflectivity is high (as from snowcover, for example). So when applying this chart to solar applications, adjust for tilt, orientation with respect to due south, time of day and time of year. If there is no persistent pattern of morning or afternoon cloudiness, incident sunlight is symmetric about due south in the Northern Hemisphere. (Consult the bibliography at the back of this book for details.)

Note, too, that some radiation data are questionable since the solar sensing network incorporated inaccuracies in certain years, and the data have been restructured using estimates of the causes for the discrepancies. How to access and types of data available are described in the appendix.

This chapter and the following chapters on wind, hydro, ocean, and wood energy are devoted to filling parts of the weather puzzle between two climatic measuring points, as well as presenting the larger scale version of climatological maps.

The seasonal change in solar radiation received is the most obvious example of how energy at a particular location varies. Areas at lower latitudes receive more direct solar radiation on an annual basis, but this value, which decreases as you move northward, is not the only consideration. South facing mountainsides receive more radiation than nearby "nonaligned" mountainsides. Likewise, southern locations which pass the latitude test can score lower due to weather factors and, therefore, experience less radiation than areas farther north.

The large scale distribution of fair weather high pressure zones near 30°N, combined with the low latitude factor, presents a zone of high solar input. But in the South and

Southeast, moist air overlying warming land is lifted, particularly during summer, by convection currents and clear skies soon are dotted with small clouds above the rising currents. Convection currents lift moist air skyward to a point where cooling produces saturation, condensation, and perhaps precipitation. This doesn't happen in the Southwest where extremely dry or sinking air precludes condensation (See Chapter 5). The result is that less radiation is received each year in the South and the Southeast than in the Southwest. As we shall see, the Southwest passes several other tests for atmospheric clarity and wins the title of prime location for solar energy receipt, although that is not the only criterion for practicality of solar energy in a location.

All southerly locations are subject to another weather factor that vastly enhances solar potential: namely, the normal track of low pressure areas. During the cold season, most lows travel from the Pacific Coast, north of San Francisco, east and southeastward to the lower Mississippi Valley and then northeastward, exiting the United States north of Cape Hatteras (Figure 4-11). One pressure system does not always make the entire journey. Instead, new systems develop or old ones regenerate in the lower Mississippi Valley and head northeast.

Alongside and to the North of these tracks, cold season cloudiness is most common (Figure 6-3). Since this zone marks the domain of colder polar air, snowcover is frequent and solar collectors which use reflected components are more effective in winter. An additional tilt of ten degrees toward the vertical is one way to take advantage of this enhancement of incident solar energy by highly reflective ground cover (Figure 7-7).

To the south of the normal low track, cold season weather usually is interrupted by brief frontal passages. Being of short duration, their effect on insolation is less important than the air mass that lies to their south, which usually is moist, tropical air.

We have already discussed the dry Southwest. Moist Pacific air incursions are infrequent there. But from Texas through Florida, a more common moisture source is the Gulf of Mexico. Moisture bearing winds flowing northward into passing lows provide one of the ingredients for clouds. The

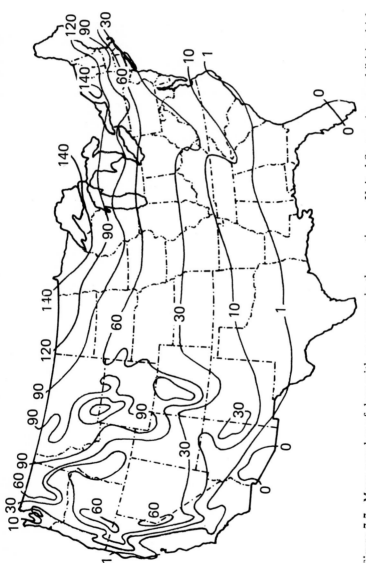

Figure 7-7 Mean number of days with snowcover in the contiguous United States. Areas exhibiting high values may experience greater reflected components of solar radiation. They also display enhanced nighttime radiation (radiational cooling) and lower daytime high temperatures (solar component reflected and not used to heat the atmosphere). Locking of water in the snowpack is also maximized here, diminishing cold season hydroelectric potential until spring.

other, cooling to saturation, is the result of convective currents over the landmass or nighttime radiational cooling which can produce persistent low clouds or fog, especially during cold season (Figure 3-4). Fogs usually burn off during the morning hours as the sun heats (and dries) the air, but then convective cloudiness appears during midday.

The nighttime sky cover serves as a blanket, diminishing the amount of heat radiated to space and thus maintaining warmer temperatures. To the north, this happens less frequently since cold, dry air is drawn across the regions by lows and tailgating polar high pressure areas. Nighttime weather regimes during cold seasons produce two results; one is a diminished heating requirement across the South and the other is an increased heating requirement across the North. But daytime weather regimes tend to offset the inequities. To the north, clear polar air is great for solar collection. To the south, daytime heating acts on moist air and rapidly obscures the sun with afternoon convective clouds. It appears that collector orientation east of south is a good idea in many of the Southern states to take advantage of radiation before the midday cloud development which persists until sunset. As we shall see, the pattern is enhanced and develops northward during warm season, suggesting orientation of collectors somewhat east of south for maximum efficiency farther north as well.

Convective clouds, signaling vertical motion in the atmosphere, are harbingers of yet another weather event, the sea breeze (Figure 7-8). Morning sun creates sensible heat over land. Land heats (and cools) rapidly since only the uppermost layer of land is involved; the radiation absorbed in nearby water is dispersed through the depths by mixing. An unequal pattern of rapidly heating land and slowly warming water produces a daily pattern that occurs periodically throughout the South during winter and is widespread across the country during summer. By late morning, the sky is filled with puffy convective clouds, except over the water where vertical motions are negligible. It is not uncommon to see a sharp line of clear sky delineating the coastline and extending seaward or lakeward. In the absence of stronger ambient airflow induced by nearby pressure systems, cooler air over the water moves inland to fill the void created by rising air. This sea breeze, cutting convective currents as it flows inland,

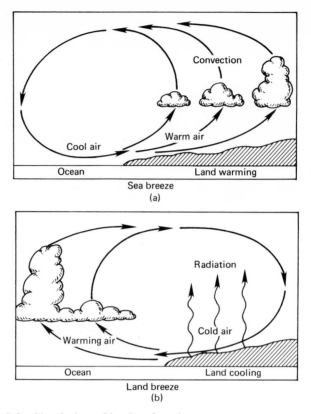

Figure 7-8 Circulation of land and sea breezes.

finally succumbs to heating and rises to form a weak front
of thicker clouds, the sea breeze front. Driven by increased
insolation as the sun gets higher in the sky, the seabreeze
speeds up and penetrates farther inland before rising. The
depth of penetration, marked by the cloud line, moves
inland, followed by the clear skies peculiar to the cooler sea
breeze air. Late in the day with lower sun angle, heating is
diminished, the driving mechanism is lost, and winds drop to
calm. Inland clouds then dissipate, permitting nighttime
radiation which reverses the airflow. Rapidly cooling land
and adjacent atmosphere are now situated alongside relatively warmer water and overlying atmospheres. Rising air
over the water invites a cooler land breeze which flows seaward until it rises to form clouds offshore.

This satellite view of the Florida peninsula (looking south) reveals convection currents rising above the land, cooling to saturation, and producing cumulus clouds. Lack of cloudiness over the relatively colder ocean waters and in spots over inland lakes sharply defines the surface below. As seabreezes become pronounced, clearing will penetrate farther inland.

Cold ocean currents off California preclude this nighttime reversal. This one-way event brings fog inland through San Francisco Bay and other coastal mountain passes. The hitch-hiking fog, as discussed in Chapters 6 and 8, resides for the night and burns off with the morning sun; then the cycle is primed for another event. Sometimes the fog persists, no sea breeze develops, and bad weather prevails until a passing pressure system induces windflow or sends drier air into the region to dissipate the fog.

Sea and land breezes only exist with low speed winds; stronger winds diminish convection or override the entire process. They occur from several blocks to tens of miles inland depending upon the strength of the temperature gradient, terrain features, and size and temperature of the water surface. Clouds are less likely in the small scale events, but even over an average sized lake you will see diminished cloudiness above and downstream. Sea breezes do battle inland against ambient airflow, but this modifies their speed, direction, onset, and demise, and the distance of inland penetration is diminished.

The inland cloud line where the sea breeze ends is a zone of reduced insolation during the prime solar hours; the cleared zone between this sea breeze front and the coast is an area of greater insolation during those hours. Where offshore fog is prevalent, the cleared zone is subject to increasingly hazy conditions as fog development diminishes insolation. At urban coastal locations such as Los Angeles, New York, and Boston, the haze is offset somewhat by the sea breeze, which sweeps air pollution inland to the front, thereby negating a cumulative effect in the city. But at the front, salt air haze and atmospheric pollutants combine to reduce insolation even further than what might be expected away from urban centers at the sea breeze front.

The seabreeze is important because it cools the coastal zone, thus diminishing air conditioning demand, and its two-edged sword admits increased insolation while cleansing polluted urban areas. The land breeze, drawing cooler ventilating winds from the interior, also can reduce nighttime air conditioning demand.

The *urban heat island*, a term which has come to denote the energy intensive heat generation found in and around larger cities as well as the large heat generating area of darker surface material, can affect local climate to the detriment of solar collection. Plumes of warmer air over factories, blacktop pavement, and congested city streets rise and carry pollutants downstream in the prevailing wind. Areas in and downwind from the city therefore experience diminished radiation not only from the pollutants, but also from cloudiness generated by the rising air. Since condensation requires very small particles to act as nuclei, the pollution offers a source of enhanced cloud development, which is believed to contribute to greater precipitation downwind as well.

Urban areas near a coastline are also subject to salt aerosol and more frequent sea breezes, since rising air from the city core encourages low level inflow from the cooler water environment. As mentioned earlier, the trade-off is that the salt aerosol sea breeze tends to cleanse pollutants from the city area and push them landward of the city core. However, if trapped within a basin, such as in Los Angeles, where an inversion also limits any venting or vertical escape of pollutants, atmospheric turbidity due to salt aerosol and pollutants is cumulative and diminution of solar radiation up to 30 percent can be expected. Some pollutants also react with

A satellite picture of Chicago and Gary, Indiana illustrates the development of convective cumulus clouds over the land, while cooler Lake Michigan inhibits the vertical currents needed to form clouds. Even more interesting are the bands of clouds originating over the city and extending northeastward. It is likely that pollution from factories and power plants provided condensation nuclei near the beginning of the bands, enhancing cloud formation. The bands then flow downstream with the prevailing winds.

Atmospheric pollution in Los Angeles is capped by the Pacific high and confined by mountainous terrain. Health, scenic vistas, and solar collection are adversely affected.
Photo by Peter Simon

sunlight to form photochemical smog which, when held for prolonged periods such as in Los Angeles, produces even greater sun blockage as well as health problems.

On a large scale, long-range transport of pollutants is becoming obvious. Cities such as New York and Boston release pollutants into an atmosphere already periodically loaded with pollutants from urban areas in the Ohio Valley and eastern Great Lakes.

During warm season, increased turbidity from pollutants such as sulfur dioxide or nitrogen oxides reduces insolation throughout a large area of the eastern United States. Visible from satellites, the murky air lingers for days between the Southern states and New England. There is evidence that the hazy air may even circulate in a clockwise direction, heading into the Northeast states, curving southward to the Gulf Coast, and then returning to the source region. The net effect is an even greater pollutant concentration. Increased reliance on coal, especially unregulated small scale burning, could greatly add to concentrations. Long dwell time allows the sun to "cook" the mixture and the resulting photochemical smog sharply reduces atmospheric transparency (Figure 7-9).

While pollution-prone cities receive diminished solar radiation, the urban heat island, being warmer than its surroundings, demands less nighttime heating (but more summer air conditioning) (Figure 7-10). For example, the cold season climate modification has prolonged the growing season in suburban Washington, D.C., which enjoys a two- to three-week longer frost-free span than nearby suburban areas.

Mountainous or hilly terrain also breeds clouds on the up-slope side, and if combined with frequent surges of moist air, can be expected to yield extremely poor solar collection characteristics. The Pacific Northwest is known for endless days of gloomy weather during cold season and to a lesser degree, the western sides of the Appalachians suffer the same fate. But air rushing across these barriers is dried, creating more frequent clear skies downwind. Professor Glenn Trewartha of the University of Wisconsin has named a large area of the Midwest the "prairie wedge" in response to the drying

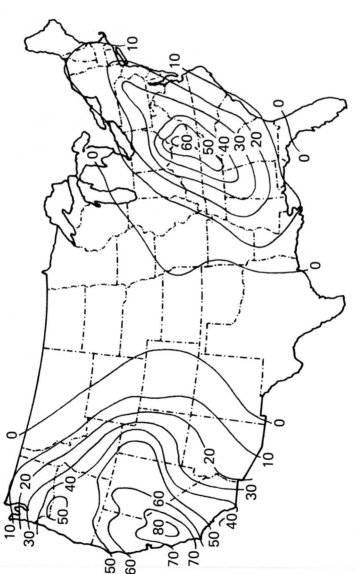
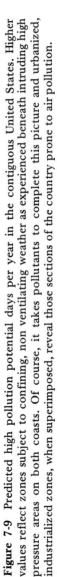

Figure 7-9 Predicted high pollution potential days per year in the contiguous United States. Higher values reflect zones subject to confining, non ventilating weather as experienced beneath intruding high pressure areas on both coasts. Of course, it takes pollutants to complete this picture and urbanized, industrialized zones, when superimposed, reveal those sections of the country prone to air pollution.

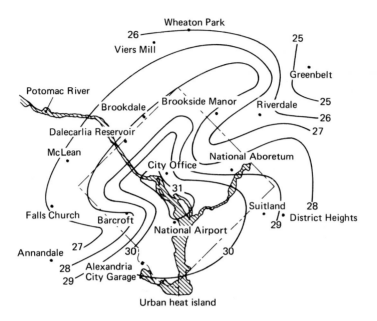

Figure 7-10 The urban heat island is delineated by the average cold season minimum temperatures (F) in and around Washington, DC.

imparted by the Rockies (Figure 7-11). Vegetation reflects the changed climate (see Chapter 11).

Being in the wind shadow of mountains can therefore be advantageous, just as sunny skies favor the wind shadow of a seabreeze, or locations downwind of water during warm season. But during cold season, colder air creates much cloudiness in wind shadows of larger bodies of water. Cold airflow over slower cooling and therefore relatively warm lake or ocean water produces much cloudiness as mentioned in Chapter 6.

Colder air occasionally creates cloudiness even in a relatively dry environment when situated above the sun-warmed earth. We have already discussed the numerous midday clouds over the humid South; drier locations also can experience these "fair weather clouds" simply because the very cold air aloft encourages additional ascent and cooling to condensation. Cloud development is most common the day after a cold

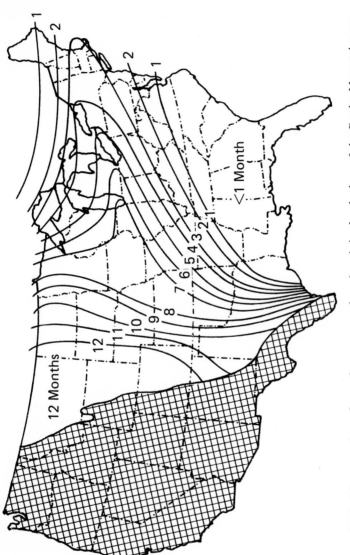

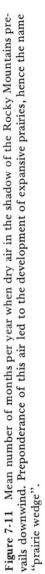

Figure 7-11 Mean number of months per year when dry air in the shadow of the Rocky Mountains prevails downwind. Preponderance of this air led to the development of expansive prairies, hence the name "prairie wedge".

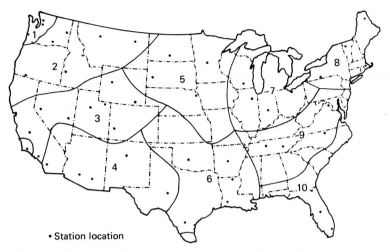

Figure 7-12 Solar climates of the contiguous United States

front passes during warm season. Cold, blue sky mornings give way to midday fair weather clouds which persist until sunset and then disappear. They develop more readily over hilly terrain due to additional vertical motions imparted there. Unfortunately in this sequence solar collection is limited, and under clear, radiational cooling night skies, heating demand is increased.

All of these factors combined present a confusing maze of pros and cons regarding solar climates. In fact, it might be necessary to look at each weather event as it applies to a site. Cort Willmott and Mark Vernon of the University of Delaware have recently completed a study which analyzes many of these events and presents a map delineating their findings. The boundaries are not rigid; each zone flows to another, but the overall picture is a bit clearer (Figure 7-12).

Zone 1 is noted for prolonged cloudiness due to frequent passage of lows and orographic lifting of moist air during cold season. Radical reversals in radiation receipt occur during warm season, when storm tracks move farther north, the Pacific high intrudes, and less frequent moist air incursions produce diminished orographic cloudiness.

Zone 2 is similar to Zone 1, but colder, drier air is more prevalent during cold seasons, promoting greater radiation receipt. During warm seasons, the locations experience an increase in solar radiation similar to Zone 1, except that these increases are greater due to distance from tracking lows and to inland location downstream from coastal mountains which have wrung water from the air.

Zone 3 also reflects warm season distance from tracking lows and diminished effects from cold season storm tracks. As a result, there is less seasonal variation in radiation here. Daily and local variations in radiation receipt are pronounced due to the extremely variable terrain.

Zone 4 is the optimum solar collecting location. Little seasonal variation and southerly latitude favor intense radiation year-round.

Warm season radiation peaks are common to Zone 5. This is the region where cold season low pressure tracks promote much cloudiness, an effect that becomes more pronounced in the eastern sections of this zone. Lying farther south, Zone 6 experiences less frequent passage of lows during cold season and sporadic outbreaks of dry air either from Zone 4, or from the back side of lows passing through Zone 5. However, proximity to moist Gulf air produces much cloudiness and fog in eastern sections. The result is decreasing cold seasonal radiation as one progresses eastward. Moist air and convective currents reduce the potential radiation in the warm season, especially during the afternoon.

Being near or north of most cold season low tracks, Zone 7 experiences much cloudiness similar to Zone 1 and, likewise, experiences a marked increase in warm season solar radiation as low tracks recede northward. Located in the foothills of the Appalachians, eastern Zone 7 is subject to upslope orographic cloudiness. Nearby downlake locations also reflect diminished solar radiation due to cold season air trajectories and increased solar potential from the Great Lakes' stabilizing effect in the warm season. But warm season radiation increases are diminished in Zone 7 by turbidity, primarily in the East where prevailing winds become laden with haze and pollution, characteristics also of Zone 9. Too, Appalachian orographic cloud cover increases, but radiation variability due to terrain is not as pronounced as in the western mountains.

Extreme variability is the pattern of Zone 8 weather, best described by Samuel Clemens' Mark Twain, whose weather forecast for most any New England day follows: "Probably Northeast to Southwest winds, varying to the Southward and Westward and Eastward and points between, high and low barometer swapping around from place to place; probably areas of rain, snow, hail and drought, succeeded and preceded by earthquakes with thunder and lightning." Proximity to passing storm systems of oceanic or continental nature, nearby mountains and ocean, and modern-day pollution trajectories are all reasons this farsighted observation holds true today.

Being on the west side of the Bermuda high, Zone 10 is affected most by warm season tropical air. Hazy, humid, pollution laden air with afternoon cloud development sharply reduces the potential for warm season solar radiation. But radiation receipt is still locally high, thanks to downslope effects of the Appalachians and the remoteness of northerly storm tracks blocked by the Bermuda high. Stabilizing sea breezes enhance solar collection near the coast.

During cold season, the northern sections of this zone exhibit a marked decrease and, therefore, seasonal reduction in radiation as southerly storm tracks exit the Mid-Atlantic states. This annual dimunition is minimized somewhat by reductions in turbidity as storm systems inhibit pollutant gathering stagnant air masses.

In Zone 10, as in the Southwest, there is high annual radiation, but nearby marine influences promote afternoon convective cloudiness and sea breezes, primarily during warm season. Moderation of local climate by these weather events, as discussed, can be important.

What all this adds up to is that, in a large nation like the United States, there is considerable variation, defying complete description, among regions in the amount of solar energy received during the course of a year. In fact, there is considerable variation from season to season and over shorter periods as well.

Several conditions in addition to the amount of sunshine received are necessary to make the use of direct solar energy practical. There must be a need for the heat. The Southwest gets more sunshine, for example, but needs less in the winter for home heating, and more in summer for air conditioning; the cold winters of most of New England, on the other hand, create a considerable demand for winter heating.

In addition, a high price for conventional fuels in the area provides a great incentive to invest in solar heating. Since the direct economic savings is in fuel that has *not* had to be burned, the amount saved each year is directly related to the cost of the fuel.

These three things — having enough sunshine, a need for the heat, and a high cost of oil or gas — together determine how practical solar heat is for a region. On this basis Boston is as good as Tucson. It has enough sunshine — 54 percent of what it would receive if there were no cloudy weather at all. It has a need for heat — the rather harsh New England winters testify to that. And its citizens pay more for the region's oil-derived electricity than those anywhere else in the country, except for New York City.

As a nation, one-fourth of the energy we use goes for heat and hot water in either residential or commercial buildings, so using solar energy for this purpose can make more than just a token contribution to the nation's energy needs.

Using Boston's climatic setting as our example, more than five times the energy needed to heat a moderately well insulated home falls on an area equivalent to the roof surface each year. We simply have to be clever enough to use what is available, given the interruptions that climatic variables impose, in order to obtain the benefits from the sun that are there for the taking.

8

WIND ENERGY

"You don't have to be a weatherman to tell which way the wind blows." A valid observation in the near term, but only the long view will produce a representative sample of both wind speed and direction.

How much wind energy is there? Looking once again at Figure 2-9, of the solar energy reaching the earth, we see that approximately one-fifth of one percent goes into wind, waves, convection, and ocean currents. Even this small percentage is forty times the world's entire energy consumption at present. Not all of this can be used, of course. Estimates made by the World Meteorological Organization indicate the potential for 20 million megawatts of wind generated power from the world's best land sites, about seven times the potential for hydropower. In the United States the estimated potential is 1.5 trillion kilowatthours per year, or about 60 percent of the nation's present consumption of electricity.

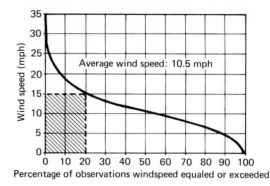

Figure 8-1 High winds occur less frequently than lower speed winds. A value between the two extremes is the optimum for wind energy.

The average available wind power at a site in the Great Plains of the United States is more than 200 watts per square meter of intercepted air current.

As for the practical significance of wind power, windmills were used in Persia as early as 250 B.C., and by the 1600s they were the major source of power for the world's most industrialized nation, the Netherlands. So there is enough wind to be interesting as a source of energy and its practicality has been tested throughout history.

Like the sun, the wind is not steady. Figure 8-1 shows a typical wind speed profile for a site in the United States. The wind blows hardest only for short periods of time averaged over a year, but slower winds blow more of the time.

The power in the wind, however, is proportional to the cube of the wind speed. This somewhat unusual relationship is not hard to understand. The energy in an imagined tube of wind blowing past a potential wind power site is proportional to the mass times the square of the velocity. In football, one avoids being hit by a fast, heavyweight lineman preferring an equally fast, lightweight halfback, because the lineman exhibits greater energy. Since power is proportional to the rate at which this energy blows by the site (many fast linemen), we need to multiply by the velocity to arrive at the well known relationship between the power output of a windmill, or wind energy conversion system, and the cube of the wind speed. Note that in spite of greater windspeeds at high altitudes, energy may be less since air is less dense aloft (fast, but light, halfbacks), therefore reducing the amount of power that might otherwise be expected.

At mountaintop locations wind speeds can reach very high values. The highest windspeed ever recorded on the Earth's surface was measured atop Mt. Washington in New Hampshire; 225-mile-per-hour winds blasted the summit in April of 1934.

Since power varies with the cube of windspeed, a site must be evaluated using more than just the average velocity. A weighted average of wind velocity must be instead considered. Imagine, for example, two wind speed profiles having the same average wind speed over a period of a month. In the first profile the wind blows continuously at the average value; in the second profile the windspeed is zero half the month, but twice the average value for the other half-month. The second profile has eight times the potential power output when the wind is blowing, and the potential to produce four times the energy of the first over the one-month period.

The cross-sectional area of wind intercepted by a windmill is proportional to the square of the windmill's radius. With these nonlinear dependences, it is clearly important to build a windmill with large blades in locations where the average wind speed is high. In fact, because of the cubical dependence on the wind speed, it is economical to invest in additional tower strength necessary to raise the windmill high above the ground; This will take advantage of the increased wind speed at greater heights where surface frictional affects are minimal. In a 30-mile-per-hour wind, a windmill with a radius of 85 feet will produce 1,000 kilowatts. But if the wind is 20-miles-per-hour and the radius 60 feet, the power output drops to 148 kilowatts. Put into monetary terms, at 8 cents per kilowatt-hour these examples would yield electricity worth $57,600 and $8,525, respectively, per month.

Again, like the sun, the wind's energy is not distributed evenly over the earth. The planet's overall circulation patterns, discussed earlier, give some clues about the best locations,

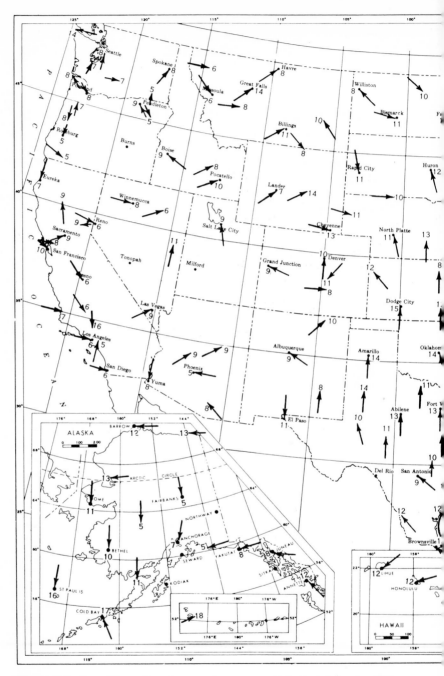

Figure 8-2 Prevailing direction and mean speed (m.p.h.) of wind, annual.

NOTE:
Arrows fly with wind.

but topographic features also play their part. Lacking adequate climatological records, we might recall local wind conditions after having resided at one location for a period of time. Most of us have an idea of the direction from which the strongest, if not steadiest, winds come.

The best bet is finding the nearest wind recording station, because proximity to an intended wind energy site is of paramount importance. The major sources of this basic information include National Weather Service sites, power plants, universities, pollution measuring sites, fire towers, factories, and various government and military agencies, especially those involved in aviation. Care should be taken in accepting wind speed data at face value since siting of anemometers to measure windspeed may be dictated by nearby obstacles. Figure 8-2 shows the mean annual wind speed in miles per hour and the prevailing direction at airports throughout the United States.

As you travel away from the nearest recording station, meteorological knowledge becomes increasingly valuable since it helps you make an educated estimate of what type of wind to expect. Beyond this, environmental signatures can give clues to local winds. Deformed trees and eroded land have tales to tell.

Two categories of windflow of prime concern are the larger scale as evidenced by wind trajectories encircling pressure systems, and the small, local circulations which may or may not be initiated or modified by the larger. The larger scale wind pattern in the United States is dictated by clockwise flow around highs and couterclockwise flow around lows as they travel from west to east, and by the semipermanent high pressure zones found off each coast. Airflow is most vigorous during the cold season. Where the underlying surface is smooth, the windflow is nearly circular and stronger as it flows about the low or high. Airflows over oceans and expanses like the Great Plains and Great Lakes exhibit this trait.

Where the landmass interferes with the larger scale flow, the river of air is acted upon by the underlying surface and turbulence is created (Figure 8-3). Like the rapids in a river, this

Lack of growth on the upwind side of trees can be an indicator of prevailing wind direction as well as speed. "Flagging" is not always a sure
indication especially at low windspeeds, and should be examined carefully. In this case, prevailing winds are assumed to travel from left to
right.

also produces zones of faster flow and greater energy. Increased surface friction causes greater variation in windspeed
and direction (Figure 8-4). Therefore, irregular terrain calls
for detailed site selection study. Intruding convection currents can interfere with flow in a similar manner, and in
another case, cold settling air modifies the flow by filling
rough terrain, routing wind currents above it. These local

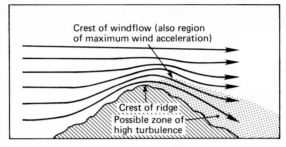

Figure 8-3 Topography increases windspeed but also creates turbulence which diminishes energy.

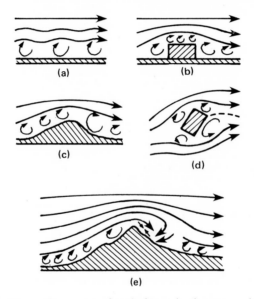

Figure 8-4 The main source of turbulence in the atmosphere is friction from the surface below. Whirls of air called eddies vary in shape and size and may occur even over relatively smooth terrain. Alternate rising and descending columns of air, caused by differential heating of the earth's surface, can also interrupt airflow creating turbulence.

wind circulations are the heart of what one must consider when locating wind energy equipment. Figure 8-2 shows the overall situation in the United States.

Semipermanent high pressure zones are found off both coasts of the United States. Their seasonal migration to the north in summer and southward in winter causes fluctuations in broad

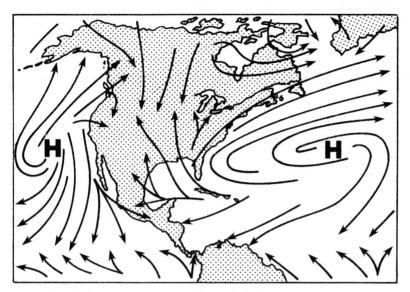

Figure 8-5 Mean warm season surface windflow.

scale windflow at adjacent continental locations. Airflow from east to west (an easterly wind) across Florida during warm season is directly related to the Bermuda high which sends these tradewinds into the Southeastern United States (Figure 8-5). This flow, enhanced by sea breezes on the Texas and Florida east coasts, creates a more comfortable coastal climate in what might otherwise be a sultry location. And, on the West Florida coast, the modifying effects of this flow diminish the inland penetration of the sea breeze. Farther north, Bermuda high circulation results in a prevailing wind from the southwest and recurrent bouts of heat and humidity in large urban centers.

Breakdown of the Bermuda high with cold season onset is attended by a less persistent easterly flow across the Florida Peninsula and a change in prevailing winds from southwest to northwest over much of the Northeast (Figure 8-6).

In the West, the cold season shrinkage of the Pacific high can be more erratic, and its wanderings are thought by some to be the controlling influence over the climate of the contiguous United States. But it is apparent that the Pacific high,

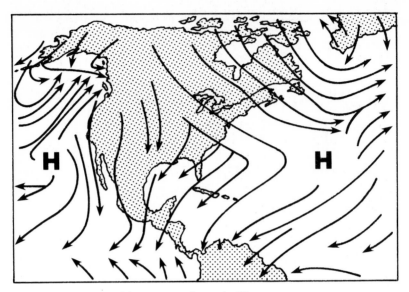

Figure 8-6   Mean cold season surface windflow.

especially during warm season expansion, creates a northerly (north to south) flow of stable marine air that parallels the coastline southward to California. Along this coast another interrelationship between the larger scale airflow and local circulation exists: the strong California sea breeze.

Ocean currents follow trajectories similar to those of the winds, circling beneath the semipermanent high pressure zones (see Chapter 10). The south-to-north flowing Gulf Stream is water driven by the wind on the East Coast side of the Bermuda high. The north-to-south flowing California current is also one segment of the driven water associated with the Pacific high. The former is a warm current, the latter cold; in fact, it is very cold during summer when the stronger high is pushing water southward — or is it? The coriolis force is at work here, too, causing the current to curve to the right. Oceanographers are aware that an even more radical right turn is taking place near the ocean surface, resulting in California coastal surface waters flowing away from the land and being replaced by waters from the depths, a process called *upwelling*. Along coasts with steep dropoffs, like the California coast, deep, cold water is drawn to the surface. During summer when hot temperatures prevail over the adjacent

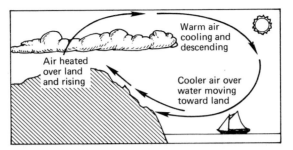

Figure 8-7 California sea breezes are vigorous due to sharp temperature contrasts between land and sea. Mountain slopes, favorably inclined to the solar beam, provide additional driving force.

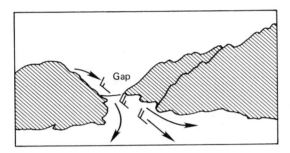

Figure 8-8 Wind speeds up when flowing through a gap. Arrows denote wind direction; the feathers indicate speed. A complete feather represents 10 knots; a half feather indicates 5 knots. A knot is a nautical mile per hour and is slightly faster than the familiar mile per hour.

land, this very cold water initiates the vigorous sea breezes propelled by the sharp temperature contrast (Figure 8-7). They may even prevail through the night.

Sea breeze speed averages 10 to 20 miles per hour and is highest during afternoon. As the driving forces are enhanced by the higher sun, the increasing speed also produces a greater coriolis effect causing the sea breeze to change direction and curve to the right. For instance, easterly Boston sea breezes rotate to a southeasterly direction as speed increases. West Coast sea breezes become more northerly with increasing speed.

Moving inland, the sea breeze encounters natural openings in the coastal mountains, such as San Francisco Bay, and is sqeezed through, resulting in increased velocity (Figure 8-8).

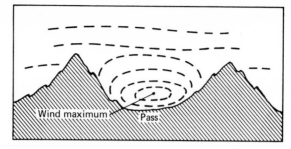

Figure 8-9 Winds rushing through a mountain pass are constricted horizontally and vertically with the highest speeds occurring in a core above and away from surface friction.

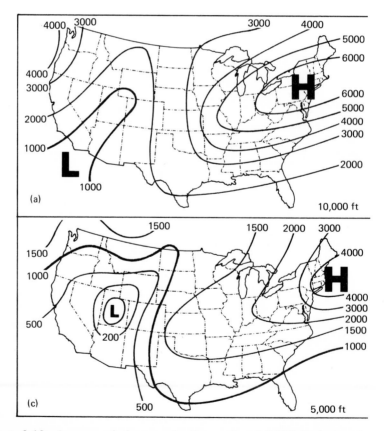

Figure 8-10 Average wind power in the west at 10,000 ft. (approximately mountain top level) in winter (a) and summer (b) and in the east

Constricting airflow through terrain features also increases airspeed between headlands at the mouths of rivers, through mountain passes, or through groups of tall buildings. Siting of wind collection devices should be considered appropriate where this happens regularly. An ideal situation would find prevailing wind parallel to the axis of a valley, pass, or inlet. Increased relief between the lowest and highest elevation would enhance the funneling effect, and constriction in the vertical, as in a mountain pass, would accelerate the wind over the highest breach in the barrier (Figure 8-9).

In evaluating constricted sites, one may note persistent driving mechanisms such as the sea breeze, or larger scale

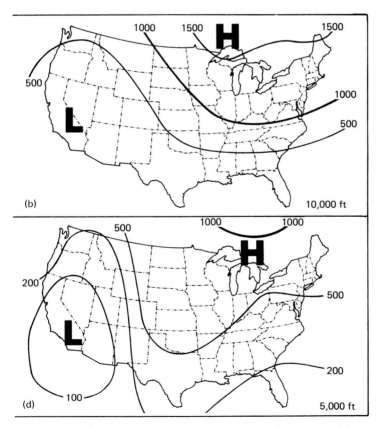

at 5,000 ft. (approximately mountain top level) in winter (c) and summer (d).

lows and highs which regularly track nearby, and infer wind direction by the circulation as it relates to the site. In hilly terrain, this judgment must be tempered by the fact that winds blow more toward the center of a low pressure area due to surface friction. Although winds tend to increase with height, they also contain less energy as air density decreases. The energy loss due to lower density would be greatest in the Western United States, since wind collection is at higher elevations, and there are less frequent visits by well developed storms with their high wind velocities. Wind energy collection at mountaintops is therefore greater in the coastal mountains of the Pacific Northwest and in the mountains of the East, especially the Northeast, where strong storms are frequent and mountain elevations lower, exposing wind energy conversion systems to more dense air (Figure 8-10).

Some valleys may be favorably oriented to increased windflow due to constriction of prevailing or sea breeze winds and another type of wind, called the mountain-valley wind (Figures 8-11 and 8-12). The latter predominates when winds are feeble and can supplement the first two as a source of energy.

Cold, clear nights in mountain locations see cool air, driven by gravity, falling down the slopes toward the valleys; this is called a *katabatic* wind (Figure 8-12). Colder snow-covered slopes enhance this wind. In valleys that open to a lower elevation, katabatic winds flow like water down the slopes and down and out of the valleys. Highest speeds are at the lower end of the valley, and increase if the valley is constricted. The flow tends to surge, with periods of stronger drainage alternating with lesser flow.

With daytime heating, drainage winds cease and an opposite flow develops. The valley, or *anabatic*, wind is most pronounced during warm season when slopes are bare and absorb much radiation if favorably inclined to the sun. Generated heat warms and drives nearby air up and along the slope. If the valley below is open on one end, a flow opposite the nighttime drainage wind travels its length. Anabatic winds are lighter and more variable, and reach highest speeds near the base of the slopes.

Mountain-valley winds are reduced and made more turbulent if the areas are heavily forested. Mountainside vineyard

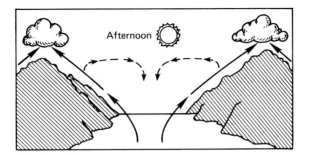

Figure 8-11 Valley winds are driven by sun warmed slopes which heat nearby air causing it to rise.

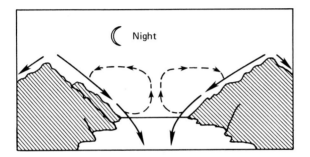

Figure 8-12 Mountain winds drain like water as cooling air falls down mountainsides and flows out of valleys. This gravity driven wind can be a reliable source of energy.

owners for instance, make a practice of planting wind-interrupting tree or shrub lines just above their locations to block the cold katabatic winds and reduce frost damage. Valleys and slopes situated above tree line experience stronger katabatic winds due to less surface friction.

The flow of air is seldom smooth. Turbulence and friction rob the air energy by reducing speed or channeling flow in rapidly changing directions. But this fluctuation or gustiness is at times beneficial, because it helps transfer the momentum of high speed upper winds to winds nearer the surface.

Diurnal changes in windspeed are a prime example of this process. Highest speeds are attained just after midday when a high sun is creating turbulent convection currents which link the upper and lower winds. At night, when convection dis-

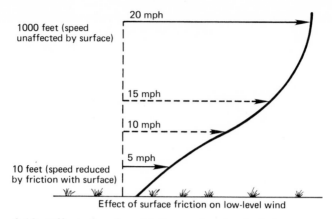

Figure 8-13 Effect of surface friction on low level wind.

appears, the link is destroyed and the friction-dragged lower level wind slows to near calm, except in cases of cities whose urban heat islands generate nighttime turbulence, or warm bodies of water which also accomplish this. Over the latter, windflow remains even stronger since little retarding friction is present. One might consider this when prospecting for potential wind sites.

The first step to avoiding high surface friction is elevation of the wind energy conversion systems. Even bare ground or water retards airflow immediately above the surface, whereas elevation of just a few feet affords considerable increases in windspeed (Figure 8-13). The rougher the terrain, the higher the retarding effect; therefore, the higher one should locate a wind device. Figure 8-14 depicts projected wind power availability at altitudes where surface friction is minimal, and enhancers such as mountains are effective. Surface friction due to trees or buildings is common to many wind generating sites. Tower heights of three times the tops of these adjacent barriers is roughly optimum, with lesser elevations producing lesser results. If turbulence cannot be avoided vertically, siting on the windward side of the barrier should be considered since a horizontal distance of only two times the height of the barrier is necessary in these cases. Downwind, a system should be located closer to ten times the height of the barrier (Figure 8-15).

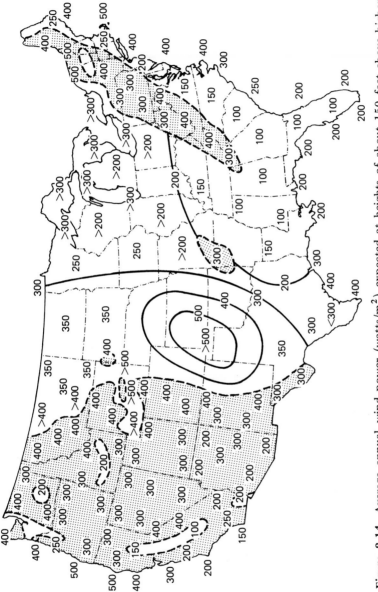

Figure 8-14 Average annual wind power (watts/m^2) expected at heights of about 150 feet above higher elevations.

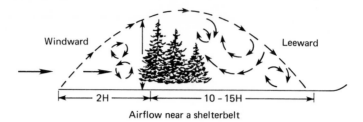

Airflow near a shelterbelt

Figure 8-15 Eddies caused by a barrier determine where wind energy gathering is impractical. The effect is greatest downwind.

Too much of a good thing is a problem when the higher speed Santa Ana winds of California or chinooks of the Rockies blast down mountain slopes (Figure 8-16). Driven by configurations of highs and lows that propel wind over a mountain range and down to the lowlands, these airflows are compressed by higher pressure, heating and drying in the process. Speeds of 50 to 100 miles per hour, particularly erratic due to gustiness, can be damaging.

Gusty winds accompanying thunderstorms also pose a threat. Thunderstorms are most likely where marine tropical air is lifted by solar heating or where cold fronts rapidly elevate a moist air mass (Figure 8-17). The first type, air mass thunerstorms, are less likely to contain strong winds. But the descending cold air within these thunderstorms, driven by falling rain, fans out when approaching the earth, producing gusty winds of short duration. Thunderstorms associated with an approaching cold front usually are organized in north-south lines and are more likely to produce strong winds, particularly in what is called a squall line (see Chapter 4).

Tornadoes, often associated with squall lines, are small, very powerful and short-lived compared to the headline-generating hurricane (see Chapter 4). Lumbering across the Atlantic, Caribbean, and Gulf of Mexico during summer and fall, hurricanes can reach a size of several hundred miles in diameter with the strongest winds usually centered about the eye and extending out some 50 miles. The eye is a region of calm and fair weather bordered by abruptly increasing wind speeds.

It is important to note that one area with greatest wind power potential — northeast coastal waters — is also prone to

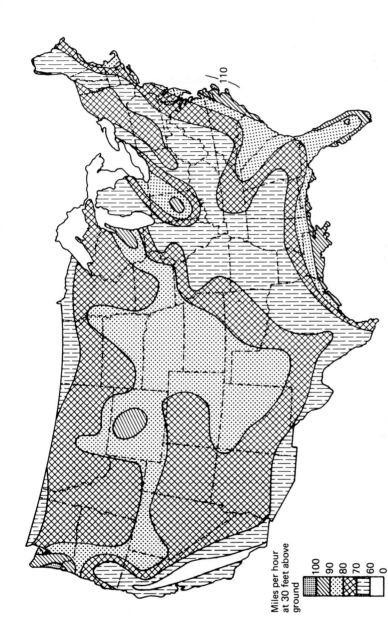

Miles per hour
at 30 feet above
ground

100
90
80
70
60
0

110

Figure 8-16 Maximum expected winds during a 50 year period. Chinooks and hurricanes account for a large proportion of the designated high wind zones.

In this satellite picture of a hurricane, the eye is visible near the center. The spiraling circulation is nearly as big as the state of Texas and rotates counterclockwise. Energy in the largest storms approaches that consumed in the entire country during 1980.

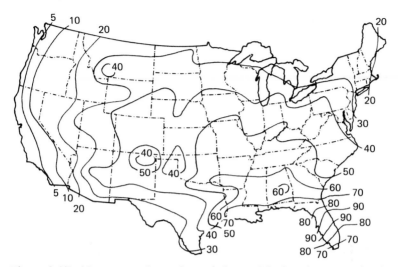

Figure 8-17 Mean annual number of days with thunderstorms in the contiguous United States.

the destructive paths of hurricanes which have moved to the United States coastline, curved northward, and exited into the North Atlantic (Figures 8-18 and 8-19). While not attaining the strength of many hurricanes, storms such as the Great Blizzard of 1978 present obstacles to the siting of wind devices in the same general area.

Annual availability of wind power as depicted in Figure 8-18 only reveals where this type of renewable resource is most likely to be found; it is not an indicator of the actual wind power which could be extracted, as other engineering considerations must be taken into account. The map is based on climatological data which for the most part represent near surface wind speeds and does not account for greater values which may be found near enhancing terrain such as mountains or at higher, frictionless altitudes. Their effects are described elsewhere in this chapter. In those areas which exhibit the greatest annual wind power potential, there is a seasonal variation which peaks during cold season. Seasonal variations within maximum zones exceed those in minimum wind power zones.

Cold season storms also present an icing problem for wind generators. Freezing rain is most common and prolonged in

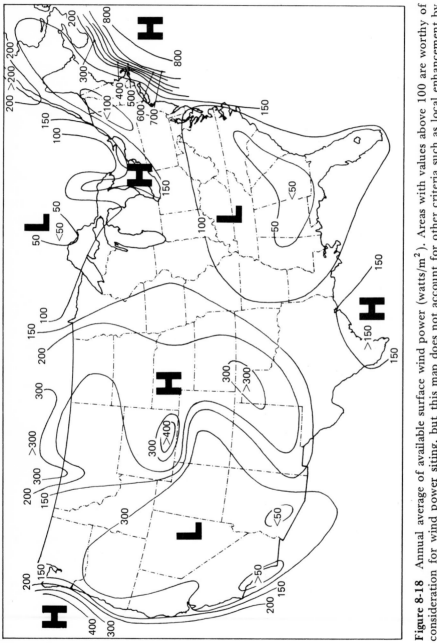

Figure 8-18 Annual average of available surface wind power (watts/m^2). Areas with values above 100 are worthy of consideration for wind power siting, but this map does not account for other criteria such as local enhancement by terrain.

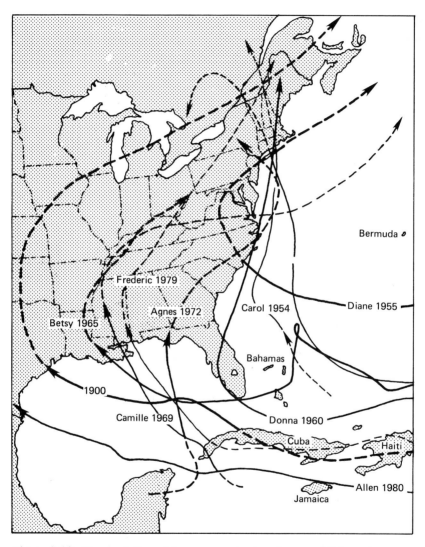

Figure 8-19   Tracks followed by some major hurricanes of this century. Rapid forward motion of storms can add velocity to already strong, spiraling winds and the coastal zone just to the right of the track is prone to the most violent weather and seas. Prolonged travel over land, especially mountainous terrain, unleashes torrential rain resulting in flooding that can be more devastating than coastal effects.

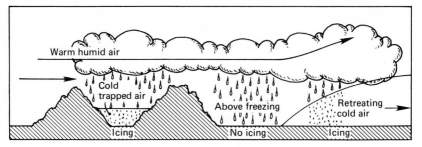

Figure 8-20 Two ways that icing can develop and threaten towers, blades and powerlines.

valleys where low lying cold air is trapped and unable to flow or mix with the winds of an approaching warm air mass (Figure 8-20). Over flatland, icing of shorter duration occurs, unless the advancing warm front stalls in the face of an intensely cold, intransigent polar air mass.

In either case, warmer rain laden air aloft drops its cargo into cold air below, causing glazing which accretes rapidly. Adding significant weight to power lines, towers, and blades, the clear ice could prove a hazard at wind energy sites (Figure 8-21). Rime ice, similar to the thin ice coating in a home freezer, is not a major problem. This tends to accumulate at higher elevations where clouds lose water droplets to any surface in their path.

From Figures 8-14 and 8-18, correlations can be drawn between wind power and demand. In general, cold season electrical heating demand coincides with high availability of wind power in areas that need it most. In the Northwest and Northeast, the front and back doors of winter storm tracks, maximum wind power and cold season peak demand correlate well. But warm season electrical air conditioning demand is not coincident with high wind power availability, especially in the Southwest and Southeast. Note the low values where power is needed most, in the hot, humid South. Coastal sea breezes present one potential solution here, and mountains offer the other.

Although Santa Anas blow during California's warmest seasons, late summer and fall, highest average wind power is ob-

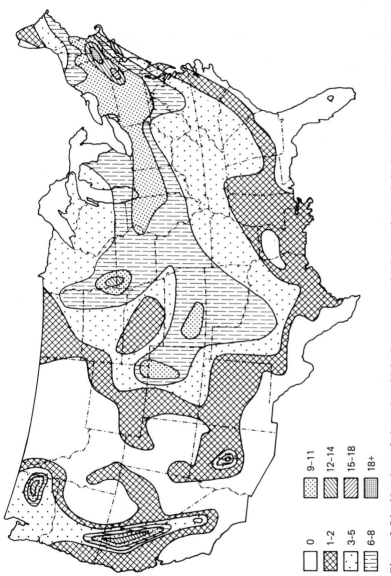

Figure 8-21 Number of times ice .25 inches or more thick was observed during a 9 year period of study by the Association of American Railroads.

served during late spring, a time of lower electrical demand. Siting to take advantage of Santa Anas is questionable, because of their variability in duration and speed. Prevalent sea breezes and offshore winds appear more closely related to high electrical demand and, therefore, offer greater potential.

Areas out of sync in the supply-demand cycle will need practical long-term storage of wind power. In the short term, areas of greatest wind power availability also exhibit the greatest variability between sites, storms, and seasons. Strong winds associated with an ocean storm in the Northeast are transitory and may or may not favor the particular exposure of a wind energy device. But airflow over smooth surfaces, such as ocean or flatlands, is seldom still or sheltered as compared to variable terrain. Wind power variance in the western maximum zones is thus greater as terrain features either enhance or reroute windflow at a particular site.

Locations subjected to high average wind speeds during cold season have higher heating requirements because winds rob dwellings of heat. In collecting wind energy, the relationship is direct; increased wind speed yields greater power for greater heating demand.

Heating degree-days are one measure used to estimate the heating demand of a structure. Unfortunately, they do not account for the increased demand imposed by a cold wind. Heating degree-days can be determined by averaging the temperature throughout a 24-hour period, and then comparing the result to a base temperature of 65 degrees. If the average is 45 degrees, for example, then the degree-days for that particular 24-hour period, equals 65 minus 45, or 20 degree days. Heating fuel suppliers and the National Weather Service keep a daily log of degree-days during cold season (Figure 8-22).

Cooling degree-days are used extensively in determining energy consumption during warm season air conditioning demand. Usually they are determined by comparing a 24-hour temperature average with a base temperature of 75 degrees. The excess above 75 is the cooling degree-day total.

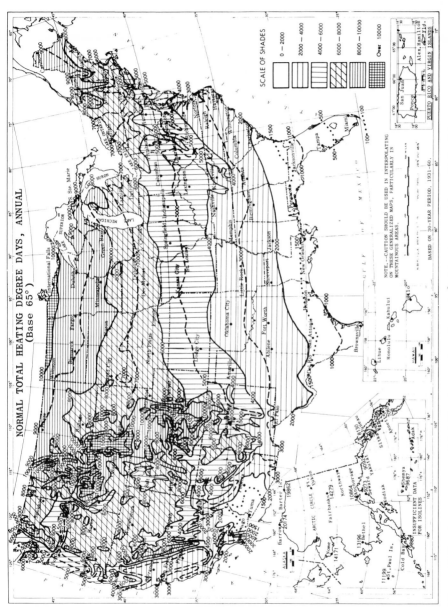

Figure 8-22   Average seasonal heating degree days (base 65° F) in the contiguous United States.

Both heating and cooling degree-days are useful in comparing the energy demands of one period with another. To arrive at an actual dollar figure, further calculations are needed and help usually is available from fuel dealers. Escalating costs of fuel complicate these additional calculations.

9

HYDRO ENERGY

From the earliest days of the water wheel, people have understood that the normal hydrological cycle can provide energy for practical use. The pattern is simple: Atmospheric circulation patterns lift water that has been evaporated by the sun at sea level and deposit it as precipitation at higher elevations. From here it runs downhill to the sea again, and in this portion of the cycle water can be harnessed to do useful work. A stream of water one square meter in cross-section flowing at the rate of 6 miles per hour, a relatively small flow, represents mechanical energy equivalent to 12.2 kilowatts.

How much is 12.2 kilowatts? As much power as is consumed by a clothes dryer, a coffee maker, a dishwasher, an electric blanket, a food freezer, a hair dryer, a stereo radio-phonograph, a refrigerator, a color television, a vacuum cleaner, a washing machine, and a water heater all operating at once!

Our intuition tells us correctly that there is much more energy in a flow of water than in a comparable flow of air. This is due to the greater density of water, so that under the same conditions of volume and speed, the mass flow of water is some 800 times greater.

Earlier generations used the energy to turn water wheels, of course, which ground corn or otherwise provided mechanical power directly for manufacturing processes. As late as 1830 the water wheel was the most powerful energy source, with the ability to produce the equivalent of 150 kilowatts in the form of mechanical energy from a large water wheel.

More modern use of this energy has been in generating electricity for wider distribution to more dispersed locations where electric motors turn the wheels of industry. Presently the most widely used form of solar energy, virtually all the hydro energy used today is made to produce electricity. Although this form of energy represents 4 percent of that used in the United States today, if all the practical sources were developed, it could produce approximately two and a half times as much energy as it now does. On a world scale, hydroelectric power generation accounts for 23 percent of all electricity at the present time; a total of 1.5 million million kilowatt hours in 1976, of which North America accounted for 500 billion kilowatt hours.

The most familiar hydroelectric installations today are the large reservoirs created by dams in various parts of the country. Where the conditions are right, water powered turbines each capable of generating more than 100 megawatts can be installed. The total hydroelectric power production capacity in the United States today is 70,000 megawatts; this is estimated to be 40 percent of the potential capacity if all practical sites were developed.

The kinetic energy in a river also can be put to practical use. Ram pumps were once very common pieces of equipment, for example. These mechanical pumps used part of the energy in the flowing river to pump water uphill from the river itself. There is renewed interest in these and other hydro sources of energy typical of an earlier day. The fact that they are not common now is not a good indication that they have

Located far from water rich regions, Hoover Dam relies on the large drainage system of the Colorado River. High evaporation rates in this arid land of continental tropical air diminish the effectiveness of large reservoirs in not only power generation, but storage for irrigation.

become outmoded. It merely reflects the convenience and the relatively low price of oil for so many years that led us to adopt machinery more appropriately adapted to the use of the stored chemical energy in this easily obtained fuel. Now, because of the convenience of electricity and the relatively widespread availability of "low head" sources of hydro energy, the renewed interest in hydro is taking the form of hydroelectric systems that operate at relatively small differences in elevation between the higher and the lower of two bodies of water (i.e., "low head").

In this method of power generation, a naturally occurring flow of water may be dammed to create a small reservoir, or may be used merely by placing an inlet to the hydroelectric turbine upstream at higher elevation. It is suitable in many more locations than the larger reservoir or "high head" installations typified by Hoover Dam on the Colorado River.

A purely artificial version of hydroelectric power called *pumped storage* is presently used by power companies for a specific purpose. Large power generating stations, whether fossil or nuclear powered, cannot be turned on and off rapidly nor would this be economical once the investment in the capital equipment has been made. But electrical demand is not steady; it undergoes wide fluctuation from season to season, and even within a 24-hour period.

To make economic sense out of these two facts, the excess power generated at certain periods by a large power station is sometimes used to pump water uphill to a reservoir; later this water is allowed to flow downhill again, generating electricity in the process. The overall efficiency of this complex intermediary process is high enough to make the technique more economically attractive than trying to match the output of the base plant to the demand, so the process is presently used where topographic features and land use patterns are favorable.

Two-thirds of the energy used to fill the upper reservoir is recovered as electricity when needed. Obviously this method can be used to overcome to some degree the failure of nature to provide enough precipitation where it might be used to generate power.

The method does not have much potential beyond its present use. There is a shortage of suitable sites and bodies of water, and there also are environmental considerations. Less than 2 percent of the electrical energy in the United States is obtained from pumped hydro storage, and this is not likely to increase much.

One interesting form of hydropower now under development, which actually depends less on weather than on the return of water to the sea, is a method that makes use of osmotic pressure. When salt dissolves in water, some of the chemical energy represented by the bonds between atoms in the salt crystal is liberated. Fresh water and salt water on opposite sides of a membrane which allows water, but not salt ions, to flow through it will have different energy levels; this shows up as a difference in height between the water on the two sides. At places where fresh water flows into the oceans, this could be used to create a difference in height of as much as 200 meters, and hydroelectric power could be then generated in the usual way using the difference in height. Concentration of salinity by evaporation could yield even higher equivalents. A brine pond contrasting with sea water could produce this energy, and would make most sense at coastal locations favored by sunny, dry weather (more evaporation to increase salinity) such as that in the southwestern United States (Figure 9-1). If it proves to be practical and environmentally acceptable, the technique could produce as much as 100,000 megawatts of electric power, if used at the mouths of all the major rivers in the United States. This is roughly 30 percent of the present generating capacity of the United States.

As we discussed earlier, cold season precipitation is most likely where the influence of orographic or low pressure systems, or both, are common in a moist environment. The two air lifting mechanisms produce a more constant water supply than another lifter, the heat of the sun, which causes air to rise and fuel scattered showers with brief, heavy downpours. There is an exception during warm season when convection precipitation becomes a major source of water east of the Mississippi River. The ability of warmer air to hold more water vapor accounts for the drenching, numerous showers which form in a humid air mass born over the waters of

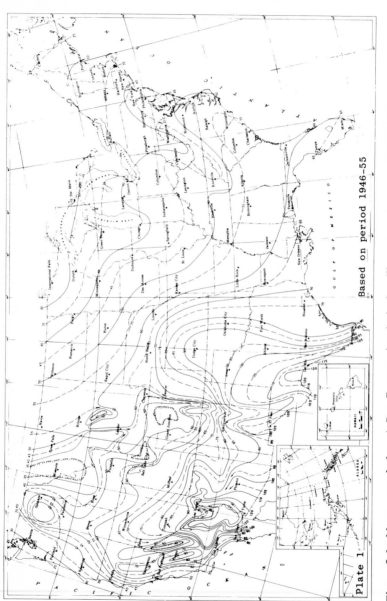

Figure 9-1 Mean annual class A Pan Evaporation in inches illustrates where, on average, laundry dries faster, river and reservoir water is lost rapidly, and evaporative cooling is facilitated.

the Gulf of Mexico and South Atlantic. Orographic influences of the Appalachians enhance these totals. A review of locations which experience both orographic and low pressure system precipitation should then reveal those sections of the country which are most favorable for cold season hydroelectric power. So regions of greatest annual precipitation/hydro potential should be evident.

In addition, consider the locking of precipitated water in the form of snow or ice, most evident at high elevation and northerly latitudes. Storage diminishes flows during the cold season, but release through spring runoff provides a more steady source of power during a longer period of time before dry weather causes streams to ebb (Figure 9-2). Other water storage, as in reservoirs, lakes, or behind dammed rivers, also distributes flow over an extended period of time. In dry environments, though, evaporation from the reservoir plays a major role in reducing the efficiency of usage (Figure 9-1).

To better understand flow potential, consider a hypothetical river basin located at a northerly latitude in mountainous terrain. The northerly location, near storm tracks for a longer portion of the year, ensures more prolonged precipitation than another site farther south. Near the sea, moisture bearing winds also would present more orographic precipitation over a longer period of time than an inland site. Locking up water in the form of ice and snow would lower runoff during cold season, and augment flow during warm season onset, until this frozen supply was exhausted. But the ebbing of flow would not be as severe as that at an inland southerly location where evaporation and less rainfall occur. Continued orographic effect and occasional nearby storm tracks would augment the precipitation. Runoff would appear as in Curve C in Figure 9-3.

If the river basin were not in the mountains, but still at a cold northerly latitude, flow would appear as in Curve B, where runoff would not be delayed and ebb would be more severe due to the lack of orographic input. In fact, hydro power generation is subject to this and to numerous examples of river basin runoff regimes, which contribute to the total flow of the river system while becoming indistinguishable after they have entered the larger artery (Figure 9-2).

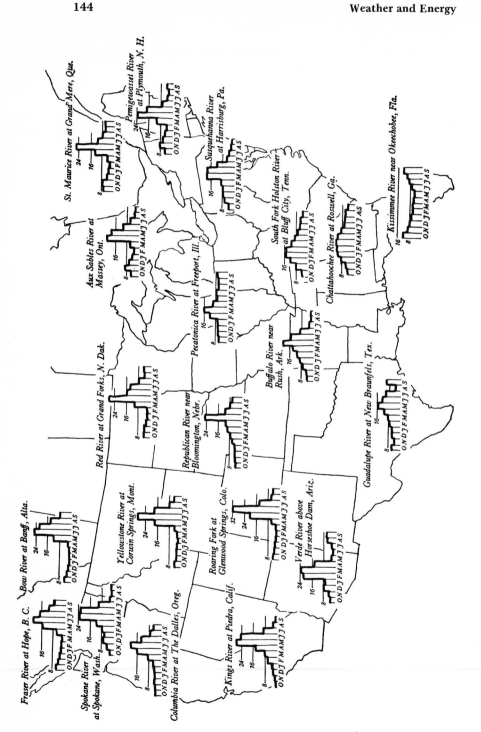

Figure 9-2   Normal distribution of runoff by months for selected rivers. Note sharp spring increases near mountain drainage basins after winter locking by ice and snow. Concave tracing of Florida rivers coincides with increased convective precipitation experienced during warm, humid season. (*From* Water, 1955 Yearbook of Agriculture)

Hydroelectric plant siting already reveals a pattern of locating near wet mountainous terrain which is also frequented by storm passage. The most obvious sites from Northern California to Washington State already are highly developed.

Another prime location, mostly Tennessee Valley Authority land, includes the drainage system of the southern Appalachian mountains. And another sees clustered hydro plants in the vicinity of the Ozark mountains of Arkansas and Missouri. All of these locations present elevations to moisture bearing winds and passing storm systems during an extended portion of the year. But one as yet poorly developed area teems with water wheels and generators of bygone mills and factories. New England's hilly terrain meets the established criteria, and is seeing a resurgence of interest in this energy source with 30 percent of its hydro potential currently developed. That

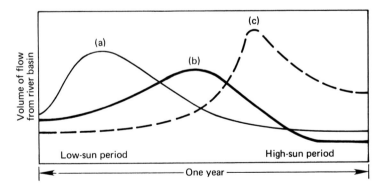

Figure 9-3   Several river runoff regimes. (a) River basin which receives precipitation throughout the year (most in Winter) with little locking of water during cold season and diminution by evaporation during warm season. (b) River basin at northerly latitude away from mountains, cold season locking, and a precipitation minimum during warm season. (c) River basin at northerly latitude or mountain location with cold season locking and warm season precipitation due to nearby storms and/or orographic effects.

The Big Thompson Project in Colorado transports water from wet upwind slopes to drier areas in the rain shadow to the east of the Rockies.

leaves nearly 2,600 New England dams and reservoirs without hydropower application, and the Army Corps of Engineers estimates that over 600 new potential sites could be developed. Producing 6,000 megawatts of power, about as
much as five nuclear power plants, they could save the six-
state area nearly 40 million barrels of oil a year.

Of greater interest is the potential for development of small
scale hydro in rural areas. In many cases across the counry,
dams or small reservoirs already exist. It is estimated that
some 48,000 demonstrate hydropower potential, and could
save over one-half million barrels of oil per day. Far from
urban power sources, often located in hilly, less developed
terrain where orographic rainfall is abundant, the numerous
sites could provide needed energy, though it would be variable because small drainage systems flood and ebb in periods
of days, as opposed to larger systems which may vary only
with the seasons.

Unlike flatland river system hydro plants, sites in the Ozarks
and Appalachians experience prolonged flow as warm season

approaches, and increasingly moist convective/orographic precipitation from the Gulf of Mexico augments that lost to retreating storm tracks. Midwest river hydroelectric plants are quite susceptible to early flow ebbing as low pressure areas cross higher latitudes, and the dry prairie wedge shadow of the Rockies prevails. Increased evaporation is also a factor here because the climate is relatively dry.

As we have seen in previous chapters of this book, moisture-bearing winds have a tendency to release much of their rainfall on the upwind side of mountains and then descend as dry chinooks after crossing the ridge line. But spillover provides a small percentage of water to the drainage area on the downwind side of mountain ridges. Drifting snow also spills over, but the total of both is not enough to balance the much greater precipitation on the upwind side. Therefore, drainage basins are endowed with greater long-term and continuous water supply if they are situated upwind of ridge lines.

10

OCEAN ENERGY

The fluid seas, giant solar collectors, are situated beneath the solar driven weather machine, and circulate around the planet in a manner not unlike the atmosphere above. Both transfer excess heat from the tropics to the deficient poles. Just as the sunshine makes the wind blow, it also makes the oceans flow. Color pictures of the earth from space show its ocean surface to be black; a sign that most of the sunshine falling on this 70 percent of the earth's surface is absorbed.

The most noticeable ocean currents shadow the semipermanent high pressure zones of the atmosphere near 30°N. The Bermuda high in the Atlantic dwells above a clockwise ocean gyral that flows northward off the east coast of the United States, crosses to Europe, turns southward to African waters and then swings westward to the Caribbean. Mariners have used this current and the winds that drive it for centuries of travel between the old and new worlds. In the Pacific, a similar circulation exists beneath the Pacific high pressure zone (Figure 10-1).

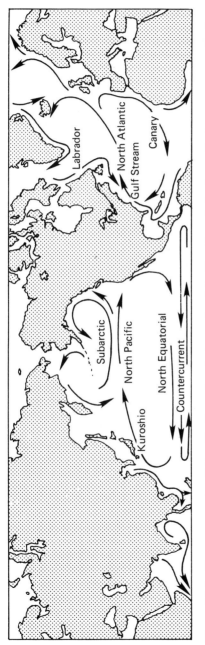

Figure 10-1 Ocean currents of the Northern hemisphere circulate like the winds above. Both serve to transfer heat energy from the tropics to cold northern latitudes.

The Gulf Stream, the western portion of the Atlantic gyral, is perhaps the best known current and carries warm tropical water northward. Modifying the overlying air, the warm water provides warm, moist air for the east side of low pressure systems exiting the United States. The result is renewed intensity or development of storms in the coastal zone, particularly in winter when large temperature contrasts exist between continental and ocean air. As mentioned earlier, these imbalances of temperature and humidity are the driving mechanisms of storms; they contributed their part to the fury of the Blizzard of 1978.

Not only does the warm current contribute to increased potential for wind energy through storm intensification, but also its kinetic energy of motion could be tapped as a power source. A most favorable location for this would be just off Florida where the Florida current segment of the Gulf Stream speeds by at about four knots, with a flow equal to fifty times that of all the world's rivers combined. The energy in this flowing mass of water has been suggested from time to time as a source to drive a submerged turbine, which would then be used to generate electricity (Figure 10-2).

On the eastern side of the huge Pacific gyral, coastal waters of the western United States experience a north-to-south flowing cold current, the California current. We discussed this cold water earlier with regard to fog formation, upwelling of colder subsurface water, and development of the sea breeze. Cold currents are more expansive and sluggish than the concentrated, higher speed warm currents such as the Florida current.

Still another type of energy generation relies on contrasts between surface and deeper water temperatures. The greater the temperature difference, the greater the available energy. Obviously, the best place to find this imbalance is tropical or semitropical ocean, or near warm currents. Both provide solar heated surface water lying over colder bottom water which, because of its higher density, has sunk, just as colder air would.

The ocean area south of Cape Hatteras, including the Gulf of Mexico, has at least the one main characteristic necessary to

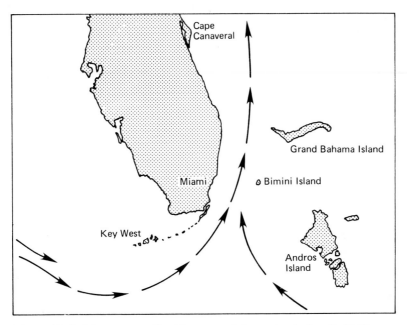

Figure 10-2 The strong Florida current is part of the Gulf Stream System and transports warm water northward. Its top speed approaches 5 knots or 6 miles per hour.

provide power from unevenly heated ocean waters: a temperature at the surface that is some 20°C (40°F) warmer than the water at a depth of two or three thousand feet (Figure 10-3 and 10-4). The acronym OTEC, for ocean temperature energy conversion, has been coined as a short way of referring to this imaginative proposal. Somewhat optimistic early estimates of the power potential from OTEC indicated that up to 10 million megawatts of electrical power might be obtained from an extensive field of plants located at various appropriate sites. This is some 30 times the present electrical generating capacity of the United States, and the estimate provided the impetus for more detailed studies.

One of the more promising approaches to development of OTEC used ammonia as a working fluid operating between two heat exchangers, one using the warm surface water as a heat source and the other using colder water from the depths as a heat sink. Liquid ammonia would be boiled as it passed through the warm heat exchanger, and the gas would be ex-

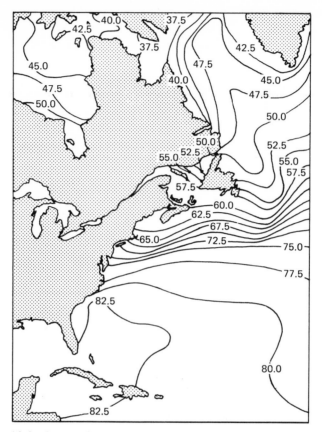

Figure 10-3 Sea surface temperatures during August. Because water reacts slowly to seasonal heating, highest water temperatures occur during mid to late summer.

panded through a turbine which drives an electrical generator. In effect this process extracts most of the energy represented by the heat of vaporization of the ammonia, analagous to the meteorological process in which the vaporized water in the atmosphere represents latent energy capable of moving air masses with great force. The ammonia is then condensed by passing it through the cold heat exchanger, and the liquid ammonia is returned to begin another round trip through the system.

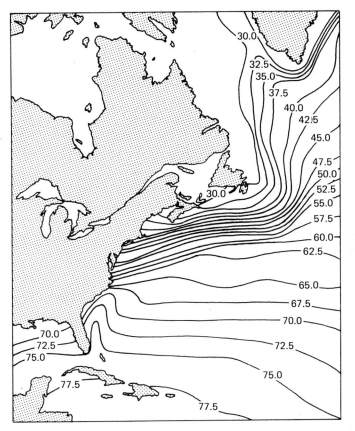

Figure 10-4 Sea surface temperatures during February. Mid to late winter is the time of coldest surface water temperatures as cooling lags behind seasonal changes on land.

There are several problems with this proposed technique. One is related to the tendency for sea animals to foul the surface of the heat exchangers. Larger animals like barnacles and mussels pose a less serious problem than microscopic organisms such as diatoms, bacteria, and protozoa. These smaller creatures produce a film on the heat exchangers and cut down the efficiency of the heat exchange process. When at the start there is only a 20°C (40°F) temperature difference in the whole cycle, this deterioration is unacceptable. Somehow the acres of heat exchangers must be kept clean in the sea water environment so they can operate at maximum efficiency. Some 400 acres of heat exchange surface will be required for a 400-megawatt power plant.

The small temperature difference available presents another challenge; namely, the enormous amount of sea water that must be brought up from 3,000 feet for the low temperature heat exchanger will require a pipe some 100 feet in diameter. Since a structure like this has never been attempted, considerable engineering development will be necessary in this area as well.

Finally, engineering problems are foreseeable with the cable that would connect the power plant with the mainland. These problems would stem from the continual motion of the floating power plant.

Given the constraints posed by the engineering requirements of OTEC, estimates of its potential have been revised. It now appears that suitable OTEC sites are limited to an area in the Gulf of Mexico off the west coast of Florida, extending north and west to New Orleans, and to several islands including Hawaii and Puerto Rico. The more realistic revisions place the potential of OTEC in the Gulf sites at between 10 and 30 thousand megawatts, roughly 10 to 30 percent of the requirement for the entire southern and southeastern region of the United States — still a considerable resource. And the cost of power generated by this technique is estimated at between 56 and 96 mills per kilowatt hour. This compares with estimates of 55 to 60 mills for new coal fired plants and 30 to 70 mills for new nuclear plants.

Among the advantages of OTEC are the facts that the method does not emit pollutants into the atmosphere as more conventional power plants do, and that power is available on a continuous basis. In effect, the vagaries of weather have been removed from the picture by the heat storage system represented by the ocean mass.

Waves are another weather induced phenomenon which can be used to generate power. Waves begin as ripples pushed by winds to heights which depend on wind speed and *fetch*, the distance over water that the wind blows and imparts energy. A short fetch will not allow a wave to grow to its potential height as determined by a particular wind speed. In a longer fetch, the wave will grow taller and accelerate until its forward motion approaches that of the driving wind, after which no additional energy is transferred. The fetch of prevailing winds about semipermanent high pressure systems is long compared to the fetch around low pressure systems, which is constantly changing and nearly circular so that waves radiate in all directions.

From ripples to building waves in a storm and beyond, the sea surface does not become a saber toothed tempest of great height with little separation between waves. Instead, in conjunction with increasing height and speed, another direct relationship exists; wavelength, the distance from crest to crest, also increases. As groups of waves, called *wavetrains*, move out of the generating fetch, the smaller, shorter wavelengths subside while the higher, energy intense, longer wavelengths persist. This swell rolls to distant shores where its rhythmic breaking contrasts with the confused crashing of smaller, locally generated seas. Each is loaded with energy. Rhythmic swells lift giant ocean liners. Smaller waves fall through a distance equal to the low head of a small dam, but spread across a great distance of shoreline.

Wave development and the use of waves to generate power would seem more logical and reliable in areas on the downwind side of larger ocean fetches where waves develop the greatest energy. These include the Southeastern United States coastal zone through the Caribbean Islands downwind of the "trades," and the northwestern coastal areas from Cape Mendocino, California, to Alaska, downwind of the westerlies.

A recent study indicated that wave power may be the most promising source of weather-related energy for England. Situated downwind of a lengthy North Atlantic fetch, the British Isles have an average power potential of approximately 80 kilowatts per meter of shore line. The potential for the entire 1500 kilometer coastline is estimated to be 120 million kilowatts, approximately twice the presently installed electical generating capacity of Britain.

Energy packed swells roll westward, driven by winds on the south side of the Bermuda high. Their energy potential is greatest from here, the shore of Guadeloupe in the Antilles, to southeastern coasts of the United States.

Large waves of shorter duration appear, as they did in the Blizzard of 1978, when strong storms enter and depart the country. New England wave energy peaks during cold season (conveniently) when Atlantic storms pass nearby, coincident with electrical demand in the region. This is also true in the Pacific Northwest, where this wave action is augmented by the waves generated in the longer fetch of the prevailing westerlies.

Tides are another possible source of ocean energy, but their magnitudes are not entirely weather-related, except as tides are affected by passing weather systems. One of the reasons the Blizzard of 1978 caused so much coastal damage is that it took place when the moon was full, so that tides were at their high for the month. In addition, the low atmospheric pressure at the center of the storm caused even higher tides, because the higher atmospheric pressure in surrounding areas exerted pressure on the surface of the ocean to cause the water to rise where the atmospheric pressure was lowest.

Weather systems, or lack of them, have another effect on ocean surface water. The salinity of ocean water varies; it is higher where the evaporation rate is greatest, and lower where abundant fresh water sources like rain or rivers dilute the salt concentration. The greater of these salinity differences represents potential energy between the differing densities of the two saline solutions. Like the "head" created by a dam, the contrast may potentially be exploited by an extension of presently existing technologies to produce energy for practical purposes. (See Chapter 9.)

11

WOOD
ENERGY

"The more things change the more they remain the same" goes the old saying, and in some respects we are seeing a return to earlier ways of doing things in an effort to solve our energy problems. A return to the use of wood in several forms in this country provides one example, although the degree to which we can improve on older methods of burning wood is surprising, given the length of time it served as a major source of energy.

In the middle of the nineteenth century, wood accounted for more than 90 percent of the energy used in the United States, although by the close of that century it had largely been replaced by coal. Most countries in the world, and approximately 90 percent of the people in developing nations, still depend on wood for heating and cooking. Half the world's harvest of wood at present is burned as fuel; the other half is used for many industrial purposes. The United States consumes 250 million tons of wood each year, nearly two-thirds for structural materials and the rest for fiber-based products like paper and cardboard.

In a broader view of the wood energy potential, each year the world's forests produce roughly five times the world's use of energy in 1975, which was 230 thousand million million Btu, or 230 quads. Not all of this is accessible for practical use, of course. It has been estimated that the power equivalent of roughly twice the electrical generating capacity of the United States could be derived economically from the world's forests on a continuous basis, since the forest replenishes each year what has been harvested. Furthermore, if modern methods of forest management were practiced more widely, silviculture, the forester's equivalent of agriculture, could triple the output of the commercial forests in the United States. This output could be compatible with the other functions of the forests, many of which are so basic and vital that it would be foolish to try to assign economic value to them.

For example, the world's forests play a basic part in taking carbon dioxide from the earth's atmosphere, which they use in their respiratory process, and in returning oxygen to the atmosphere as a byproduct. In this book we focus on the forests as a source of wood for energy, but it would be a mistake to develop this resource without consideration of its worth in other ways as well.

The recent rise in fuel prices revived interest in wood stoves and fireplaces for home heating. In the Northeast, the old Ben Franklin stove and some of its modern counterparts are used to reduce the strain on the family oil bill. Foundries have searched their back rooms for casting patterns nearly forgotten, and are producing wood stoves at a rate no one would have believed prior to 1973.

There is about as much heating value in a cord of wood as in a ton of coal or in four and a half barrels of oil. The cord is a measure based on volume; it is a rectangular stack 8 feet long, 4 feet high, and 4 feet wide, or 128 cubic feet as piled, of which approximately 70 percent is wood, the rest spaces between the pieces. This is the roughest of comparisons, because the heat value of wood depends on the type of tree

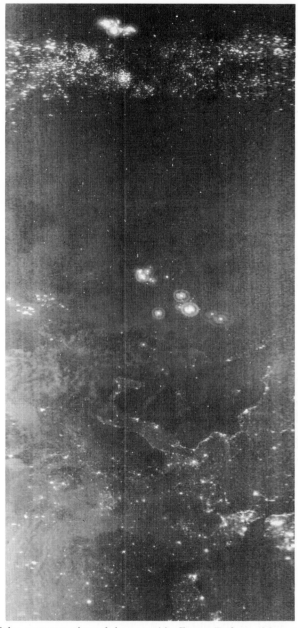

Major light sources viewed by an Air Force Defense Meteorological Satellite. At the top, Italy's boot and the lights of European cities. In the middle, gas flares at oil fields in Algeria, Libya and Nigeria. And below, the Milky Way of lights emanating from fires across Africa. This extensive burning of tropical forests could alter the climate of the planet.

and whether the cut wood has been allowed to "season" so that most of the moisture has evaporated. The chemical analysis of moisture-free wood is about 50 percent carbon, so the use of wood as a fuel is one of the few solar energy sources that releases carbon dioxide to the atmosphere as a product. However, since the tree extracted carbon dioxide from the atmosphere during its growth phase, the net result on the atmosphere's carbon dioxide load is, at first approximation, nil. There is growing concern that destruction of world forests might change this natural effect and contribute to an increasing concentration of atmospheric carbon dioxide. Clearing of forest land for timber, development, or more primitive slash and burn agricultural techniques is widespread. Indeed, nighttime satellite pictures show a darkened planet girdled by a Milky Way of flickering wood fires in tropical regions where clearing and burning is most prevalent.

Fossil fuels once were growing organic matter, too. At some time long ago they extracted carbon dioxide from the atmosphere, but the cycle of extraction and return in the case of fossil fuels takes place on geological time scales, instead of decades. Over the time span of interest to present civilization, the burning of fossil fuels adds to atmospheric carbon dioxide content; the burning of wood, if the forests are replenished by adequate management, adds considerably less to the atmospheric load of carbon dioxide. Furthermore, wood contains no sulfur, as do coal and oil, so burning wood produces no sulfur oxides, which are among the objectionable pollutants of the atmosphere, although it does produce other pollutants.

In some areas of the country today waste products from the lumber industry are burned to produce electric power. This rather fortunate preservation of an older technology provides a starting point for us to consider the possible wide-scale use of wood for the same purpose. How to harvest wood economically for central power plant generation of electricity is one of the major problems addressed by the new technology. One of the more promising solutions is to use mobile "chippers" to reduce trees at their growing site very quickly to a mass of chips. This material is then trucked a short distance to a processing location where part of the product is burned to dry the rest. Removing most of the moisture this way makes for more economical trucking to a central location, where the wood is compressed into pellets so it can be handled more easily by automatic machinery in the power plant.

Other modern methods of extracting energy from wood and other plant products include the possibility of using them as a basis for synthetic fuels. Processes are under development for possible gasification to make a hydrocarbon fuel like natural gas, liquefication to make a petroleum-like fuel, and fermentation to produce a fuel that can be added to gasoline to extend its supply.

The production of a gaseous fuel from wood is an idea that actually has been around for decades, although newer, more efficient processes are presently under development. The use of catalysts or of higher pressures, for example, improves on the older methods to produce a gas with about one-third to one-half the heat content of natural gas.

Wood also can be liquefied by several processes which produce an oil that resembles No. 6 fuel oil, and this can be burned directly in furnaces without modification.

In another synthetic fuel process, wood can be used as a feedstock for the production of methanol, a common combustible liquid which makes "gasohol" when mixed with gasoline in proportions approximating 10 percent methanol to 90 percent gasoline. This could extend gasoline supplies by using domestic sources, although the net energy gain is not certain at this time.

Wood also can be processed pyrolytically by several methods to yield a variety of end products. One method consumes 3 tons of wood per hour and yields 40 to 50 gallons of oil, one ton of charcoal, and 7 to 8 million Btu in the form of a gaseous fuel.

How does weather affect the possibility of using wood as a source of energy? The growth of plants depends on three things: the amount of sunlight available for photosynthesis, the temperature, and how much water is available. If any of these ingredients is lacking, less growth takes place. A lot of sunlight without much water produces deserts. Added water yields grasslands. Low temperature produces tundra. Hot and

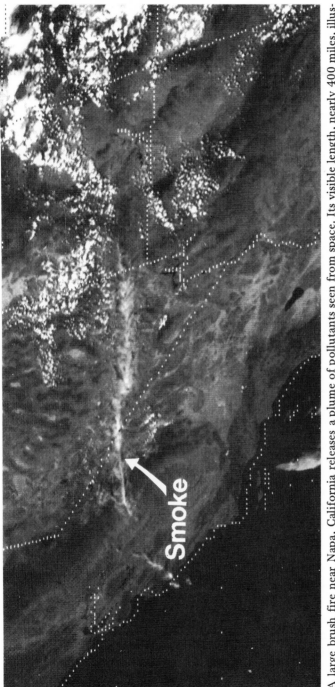

Smoke

A large brush fire near Napa, California, releases a plume of pollutants seen from space. Its visible length, nearly 400 miles, illustrates the great distance pollutants travel in the atmosphere. In the East, this approximates the distance between Pittsburgh and Boston. Dispersed, invisible pollutants travel even greater distances and similar transport is probably causing increased acidity in rainfall downwind of Ohio Valley and Midwest industrial centers. The acid rain and dry deposition of acidic particles is causing concern in the Northeast and Canada.

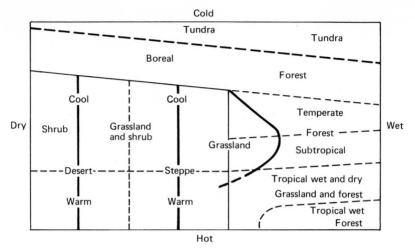

Figure 11-1 How vegetation is related to various climates. Note that this chart could be superimposed over the United States to reveal many vegetation and climatic similarities.

wet weather produces rain forest. So the seasonal distribution of sunlight, temperature, and water governs the type of plant growth that will survive and prosper in a given area. Moderately cold and wet weather is the optimum environment for forests (Figure 11-1).

The net effect of weather on plant growth in the United States is well known. The forests of the North, the savannah of the plains (prevalent before widespread agriculture changed the scene), and the extensive hardwood stands of the South were all to be expected from the adequate rainfall and the moderate temperatures of these regions. Forests are conveniently close to many population centers which have a need for wood heat.

On the other hand, the great desert of the Southwest is traceable to the way the mountainous West Coast wrings moisture from the prevailing westerlies as they are forced to rise, cool, and precipitate in their travel from the mountains to the land on the lee side. The blocking semipermanent Pacific high is another factor, especially during warm season when its enlarged circulation shunts storms far to the north. Wood is scarce here, but it is also not needed to meet high heating demand.

As sunlight reaches the ground and warms it during the day, heat is transferred to the air by convection and the evaporation of moisture. If the ground is dry, more of this energy goes into the air by convection, and as in deserts the area probably will be turbulent and windy. If the ground is moist, more of the energy goes to produce evaporation of water, and the air will be less turbulent. So the prevailing weather patterns that produced a particular plant growth in an area are then modified to an extent by the plants themselves in such a way as to promote continuation of that species.

An interesting weather related mechanism produces rapid development of a desert area once it has started. If a vegetated area is too heavily grazed or deforested, less moisture will evaporate from the sparser ground cover and less sunlight will be absorbed at ground level, since reflectance of the bare ground is greater. Dust episodes increase, and the resulting atmospheric turbidity inhibits solar radiation, thus diminishing warm convection currents which could lift air and produce rain. The result is less precipitation, which accelerates the formation of desert. Professor Reid Bryson at the University of Wisconsin has offered this explanation for the dissappearance of an early agricultural civilization from the Rajasthan Desert area of India.

Figure 11-2 shows the distribution of major forest types in the United States. Softwood conifers like western hemlock, Sitka spruce, Douglas fir, and redwood are found in West Coast regions. Ponderosa and lodgepole pines, Douglas fir, true fir, Englemann spruce, and aspen predominate in the Rocky Mountains. In the Southwest one finds pinon, juniper, and ponderosa pine, depending on elevation.

The eastern United States is characterized by mixed hardwoods like maple, beech, and birch in the northern states, and oak and hickory throughout the region. However, softwoods grow throughout the region as well. The Southern pine forest contains loblolly, shortleaf, slash and longleaf pines. White pine, jack pine, and red pine occur through the northern states of the East, and spruce, fir, aspen, and birch are found in the northernmost states. Oak, cypress, and gum also are found in the Southeast.

An interesting relationship exists between spruce and fir forests and the migrating polar front. The southernmost

Figure 11-2 Dominant vegetation in the major forests of the United States.

☐ No forest

⬚ Broad-leaved deciduous hardwoods

■ Coniferous softwoods

▨ Mixed stand of softwoods and hardwoods

extent of these forests nearly coincides with the average winter position of the polar front. Shrinking northward in summer, the higher latitude average position of the polar front nearly defines the forest's northern boundary in Canada.

On a smaller scale, exposed south facing mountain slopes exhibit drier and sunnier weather regimes corresponding to locations hundred of miles farther south. This inhibits spruce and fir forests, confining them to the higher elevations while on north facing slopes just across the valley, spruce and fir abound at low levels. Poleward facing slopes far to the south of where spruce and fir normally terminate are colder, less sunny, and wetter, and exhibit verdant spruce and fir cover. Microclimates like this may also support tree growth at otherwise untenable locations. West Coast redwood groves depend upon dense, relatively wet fogs which sweep into coastal mountain vegetation, accumulate as droplets on limbs and leaves, and drip life to roots below. Eucalyptus and pine groves even farther inland in the Berkeley Hills depend upon drip precipitation as well.

12

STORING THE WEATHER

The earlier parts of this book have explained how weather phenomena work, and how much energy they contain. We have seen that there is energy in sunlight, wind, waves, ocean temperature differences, and other weather related sources to supply our practical requirements far into the future. We have even seen that in some cases the equipment is already available, and in fact was commonly in use before the era of cheap oil.

So, what's the problem? Why don't we simply develop the devices and methods presented in previous chapters for putting this energy to practical use and forget about (or at least phase out) the present reliance on fossil fuels, which we are either depleting or find objectionable for environmental reasons?

Using each of the weather phenomena for practical purposes has its own technical difficulties, and at this level we must address each technique individually. In this chapter, we will try to put these matters into perspective.

Weather related phenomena are referred to in present-day language as "renewable" sources of energy. Perhaps "recurrent" would be a better term, since, with the possible exception of wood, no effort is required on our part to regenerate the source; it simply recurs again and again because the sun shines and the earth rotates on its axis at the right distance from the sun. Ultimately because of these two conditions, the energy sources we have been talking about are spoken of as inexhaustible. The energy contained in direct sunlight, wind, waves, and ocean temperature differences will not be depleted by their usage in any foreseeable quantity, since they recur without intervention each time the earth rotates in the shine of the sun. This is an obvious but important technical advantage shared by weather related sources of energy.

This is not to say that use of these energy sources will produce no environmental impact, of course; this question must be taken up carefully with any planned large scale use of a natural energy source. These effects have already been discussed in Chapters 7, 8, and 11 on the use of direct solar energy, wind energy, and the weather related aspects of wood use.

So what then are the technical problems with the use of renewable energy sources if they are virtually inexhaustible, recurrent, and in sufficient supply to meet practical needs? The biggest problem is that those with the greatest short-term potential, sun and wind, and the longer-term but promising ocean wave energy, are intermittent in any given location. If they are recurrent energy sources, they recur on their own schedule and not on one that is convenient. Energy is not available on demand. This, of course, is one of the main reasons fossil fuels have become so popular: the energy they contain — the release of energy that takes place when a carbon atom is burned to form a carbon dioxide molecule — can be called on when needed. The chemical energy released in burning is already stored. We must dig it up or pump it up, of course, but relatively easy digging has made these sources popular. The question sometimes asked about solar energy — "What do you do when the sun doesn't shine?" — is one which demands an answer.

The answer is that you collect it when it is available, use it at that moment if it is needed, and arrange to store the rest in some way that allows its use later. This means that any practical solar or wind system needs a storage technique or device, and the cost of the whole energy production system must include both collection and storage capability.

How do you store something as ephemeral as the weather? There are several ways. In some cases the problem can be partly circumvented. It is possible to use existing correlations between energy availability and need, to simply avoid the necessity for storage. One example has been mentioned already in Chapter 7. In a solar energy system used for air conditioning in some climates, there is a correlation between the sunniest days in the summer and the need for cooling. These are also the days with the most solar energy to provide power for the system, so in these climates the use of solar energy on a catch-as-catch-can basis may be adequate. The net effect of using favorable correlations in this way is to make it necessary to store only a fraction of the energy required, and the storage system may therefore be smaller and less costly, or even nonexistent.

In many other cases it is technically feasible to generate power in one location, convert the energy into an intermediate fuel, and then distribute this fuel for later use as needed. One of the ways to tap the various ocean energy sources, for example, is to generate electricity at the source, use this to electrolyze water into hydrogen and oxygen, and transport the hydrogen to its needed location. The hydrogen can be stored either as a compressed gas, in its liquid form at minus 251°C (-420° F), or in chemical form as a hydride.

The hydrogen is then burned later when energy is needed, making water once again (not carbon dioxide, with its possibly undesirable climatic effects), and the energy of combustion is used to perform a useful task: rotate machinery to make electricity or move a vehicle, perhaps. Or the stored hydrogen can be recombined with oxygen in a fuel cell to reproduce electricity, if that form of energy is needed. Each conversion costs something in the form of energy lost in inefficiencies and in the cost of the necessary machinery, but the whole system now meets the requirements; it can collect energy when available and deliver it when needed.

Still another technique is to generate power when it is available from one of the intermittent sources and use the existing grid network as "storage" for the excess. Wind energy conversion systems, for example ("windmills", although we don't grind corn with them much anymore), are used commonly to generate alternating current when the wind blows. After proper processing so that it meets the requirements of voltage, frequency, and phase, the generated power can be fed into the existing electrical distribution network where it adds to the electrical energy in transmission at the moment.

The large number of customers on the grid ensure that the power is on its way to a point of present demand. The inefficiencies and cost of conversion to a storable form and reconversion into electricity are avoided, and large wind generating facilities presently are among the most economically attractive possibilities for the near future.

One way to store electrical energy is to charge a storage battery. This is often the method of choice in spite of its rather high cost, because electricity can be reclaimed efficiently from a storage battery simply by completing an electrical circuit across its terminals.

Electric storage batteries are an obvious solution to the energy storage problem applicable to both small scale and larger scale needs. Lead-acid storage batteries have been used for years not only in a mobile capacity to store electric energy for automotive starting, but also for stationary industrial purposes as well. Batteries already are used for storing the electricity produced by wind energy conversion and photovoltaic systems in remote locations, but they are expensive. The cost of an automotive battery is charged off to the convenience of a self-starting automobile; but energy storage either by utilities or on a smaller scale by the homeowner must be more cost conscious.

New batteries being developed will be both less expensive per unit of energy stored, and have longer life than the lead-acid battery. The primary goals are batteries that will stand up under 2,000 to 3,000 charge-discharge cycles over a 10- to 15-year period, and cost less than $50 per kilowatt hour of storage. Among the more promising candidates is a sodium-sulfur battery, an improvement on the more common lead-acid battery. The sodium and sulfur electrodes are liquids in this new approach, and the electrolyte is a solid ceramic material. This greatly increases the likelihood of long life for the battery, although it boosts the operating temperature range to near 300°C (570°F). A zinc chloride battery also in the development stage meets the goals mentioned above and operates at lower temperatures: near 40°C (100°F).

There is another disadvantage to the need for an energy store; some energy is lost in conversion to the stored form and in reconversion to the useful, kinetic form. These losses directly affect the efficiency of the system, and require a larger collection system (with a greater investment) than would be the case if no storage were required.

The energy cost of conversion processes can be significant, even under the best of circumstances. Electricity is stored in an electrical storage battery with roughly 85 percent efficiency, for example (rather high for conversion devices), and reconverted to electricity with about the same efficiency. The storage system's overall efficiency is .85 × .85 which equals 72 percent. More than one-quarter of what was produced is lost in the storage and reconversion processes. Most devices are less efficient, so the losses connected with the storage of energy are an important part of the overall economics of the system.

For best efficiency the storage technique chosen must bear a sensible relationship both to the method of collection and to the end use planned for the energy. It would make little sense to take the heat energy collected by a flat plate solar collector and convert it into electricity for storage in a battery if the energy were needed just to heat water. The first law of thermodynamics allows efficiency to be calculated on the basis of the quantity of energy involved, but the second law of thermodynamics teaches respect for the quality of the energy. It makes better technical and economic sense to store the heat energy collected by the usual solar collector, for example, in the form of heat energy if its later use is to heat a room or to heat water.

What we are saying here is that emerging sophistication about energy use, forced by the passing of an era of cheap energy, leads us to understand the importance of considering the entire energy system from start to finish in more technically appropriate and more economic ways. One way of storing the weather will not be appropriate for all ways of collecting it or using it.

Several varieties of the flat plate solar collector retrieve energy from the sun in the form of air or water heated to 50° or 60°C (122° to 140°F). This is just the right temperature range for heating living space or domestic hot water. So thermal storage techniques are coming into existence to make use of this heat to best advantage.

First on the list is an insulated tank containing water. It is hard to beat water for cost and heat storage capacity. With a specific heat capacity of one Btu per pound for each Fahrenheit degree of temperature change, no other low cost liquids come close. Insulated tanks with water as the thermal ballast are therefore common in solar heating systems. To make the economics more attractive, there is also a developing tendency to build water storage into the structure so that the tankage performs double duty. Structural walls with water storage capacity and inexpensive underfloor storage systems that provide radiant floor heat, for example, are finding their way into the design of solar homes.

On a larger scale, the feasibility of storing heated water in specially insulated lakes is under study, as is the feasibility of using aquifers to store heated or cooled water.

When the output of a solar collector is heated air, an economical heat storage technique involves passing the heated air through an insulated bed of gravel. Very often the heated air is forced through the stone in one direction so that the warmer end is at the inlet, but heat retrieval is accomplished by forcing air through the bed in the opposite direction. This allows retrieval of the warmest air from the bed for delivery to the home.

"Passive" solar heating techniques attempt to use as few mechanical devices as possible, relying instead on the absorption of sunshine by parts of the house with thermal mass for storage. These can be water storage containers or quarry tile floors, for example, placed so that they receive direct sunshine through the south facing windows. Retrieval of the stored heat takes place by unassisted conduction and convection from the thermal mass components. Glazed living areas tend to be too hot when the sun is shining and too cold when it is not, and the trick is to mitigate the temperature excursions to an acceptable level by balancing glazed area, storage mass, heat transfer rates, heating requirements, and seasonal variation in sunshine.

Certain phase change salts are another group of materials attractive for thermal storage. These salts undergo a phase change at a temperature suitable for the delivery of heat to the house. Just as water either absorbs or delivers heat at a constant temperature as it goes through its freezing or melting phase change, salts like sodium sulfate decahydrate absorb or deliver heat at a constant temperature as they go through a less familiar phase change. The salt molecule either incorporates ten water molecules into its structure or sets them free, with the liberation or the absorption of heat at a constant temperature. Encapsulated in plastic, these salts are being marketed for incorporation into both active and passive solar structures.

On the larger scale appropriate to central power producers, pumped hydro storage has alrady been described in Chapter 9 as a method used to store excess electrical generating capacity in the form of the potential energy of an elevated body of water. Although this technique is not likely to see much expansion beyond its present use, a modification of the concept shows more promise. The newer idea involves making an underground water storage cavern in rock several thousand feet below the earth's surface. If connected with a body of water at the surface, the system is now capable of energy storage like the above ground system in current use. If it proves out, however, it should have broader applicability than the above ground system because the pond at the surface can be much smaller. The potential for greater difference in elevation between the two bodies of water makes it possible to store an equivalent amount of energy with the use of much less water. The largest surface system in use has an elevation of 250 feet above Lake Michigan; a subterranean system 3,000 feet below the surface would require a volume of water roughly one-twelfth as large, since the energy storage potential is directly proportional to the difference in elevation between the two reservoirs.

Compressed air also allows energy storage, and a technique that uses an underground reservoir as a receptacle for pumped air is currently in operation at a German electric utility. Compressed air storage is attractive for several reasons. The underground cavity required is smaller than that needed for the hydro techniques we have described, because the stored energy density can be greater with compressed air. There is a greater selection of sites because the air cavern can be either rock or salt. And the minimum size for the system to be economical is smaller than either of the two pumped hydro systems. There are technical complexities not present in the hydro systems. Since air gets hot when it is compressed and cold when it expands, the compressed air must be cooled as it is pumped into the reservoir to prevent fracture of the rock cavern or creep of the salt. Later, when the air is released to turn the turbines for electrical generation, it must be reheated at the cost of some fuel for the process. The economics are attractive for this system, however, since the smallest economically feasible compressed air system is probably less than one million kilowatt hours, as opposed to a 10 million kilowatt hour facility for pumped hydro.

Although these techniques have been developed primarily to store excess energy generated by large conventional power plants, the concepts are valid for storage of the power generated intermittently by the variable weather related energy sources, assuming these to be on an equivalent scale. Whether they can be shown to be economical on the smaller scale appropriate to residential or commercial use of these energy sources has yet to be proven.

Electricity might be stored with high conversion efficiency in superconducting circuits, possible only at temperatures in the region of minus $255°C$ ($-427°F$). The overall cost of the system puts the economic feasibility in doubt, however, even for storage systems with 10 million kilowatt hour capacity.

Kinetic energy can be stored and retrieved in flywheel storage systems. This technique has been studied as a possibility for electrical utilities; however, the cost appests too high to compete with other storage systems.

Direct sunshine and wind are characterized by variability with respect to locality, and they are intermittent on a daily basis. The energy they provide is storable either as heat, in the form of an intermediate fuel, or, if electricity, in the national grid. Hydro is variable with respect to locality, intermittent on a seasonal basis, and storable as an elevated body of water. Ocean wave energy is confined to coastal regions, intermittent on a daily basis, and storable in the form of an intermediate fuel or, if electricity, in the national grid. Ocean current and ocean thermal energies are confined to certain offshore regions, though continuously available. They are already stored, storable as an intermediate fuel or, if electricity, in the national grid.

Wood energy varies with respect to locality and is continuously available. It is already stored energy, but may be processed and stored as an intermediate fuel.

What you do when the sun doesn't shine, then, is to draw energy from the store. We have seen that a variety of techniques exist for storing the energy retrievable from weather related systems. They already represent a sophisticated blend of cost, clever use of what's already available, and consideration for timing. It is necessary to know when the energy will be needed, at what rate, in what form, and for what purpose. As we said at the beginning, there are few simple answers to complex questions.

APPENDIXES

AND ONE LAST THING . . . .
PLEASE TURN OFF THE LIGHTS

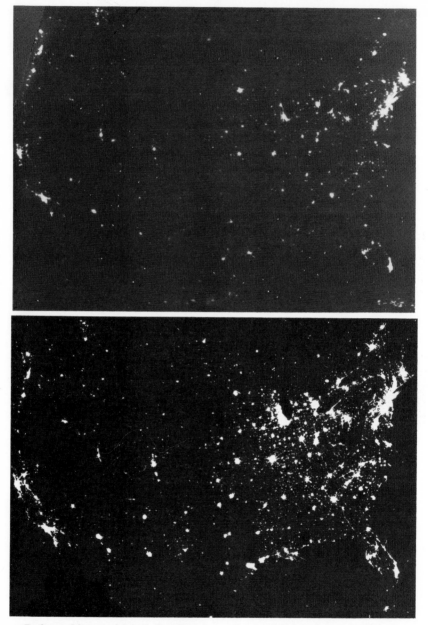

Defense Meteorological Satellites reveal a striking increase in lighting across the country between 1973 (top) and 1979 (bottom).

Appendix A

WEATHER INFORMATION

Dampened finger raised, with one eye on the barometer and the other on the clouds, old timers went about their weather forecasting ways. Today, farmers and mariners continue this practice, on the lookout for weather changes that might necessitate immediate action on their part. As we have seen in Chapter 4, barometric tendencies and wind speed and direction changes signal future weather. Adding a third signal — clouds — makes for an even more accurate forecast. But these tools are only useful in the near term, about 12 hours. Sometimes even the most modern weather equipment fails to give proper guidance for a similar period, but most of the time, forecasts of specific weather can be ascertained for a period three days ahead. A one-day forecast is *most* accurate; the longer the period, the greater the chance for error. Beyond that, the game becomes tricky, as in pinball. Multiplication of error produces greater variation after the hammer strikes the ball and sets an initial course. At first, one can plot (forecast) the ball's trajectory, but small changes in rebounds from

```
+HOURLY  10
SA   SOUTHWESTERN STATES 2B2007
ENV  AUTOB BV888 53/36/3013/994 PK WND 25 000 TL
OGD  30 SCT 70 49/29/3110.992
SLC  E45 BKN 40 121/51/34/3512/992
VEL
4HV  E70 BKN 150 OVC 60RW- 50/36/0000/977/MTN TOPS OBSCD ALQDS RB3
U28
PUC
1V1  FINO/NOSPL
EGE  E50 BKN 150 OVC 30 019/44/16/0808/9
AKO  RS 1950 W2X3/4 S-F 042/34/32/3617/964
DEN  W4X1/28-F 035/36/31/0213/967/R35RVR35
FOL
```

Sample of hourly observations taken in the southwestern states. The first three letters indicate the observation station or airport and usually appear on airline luggage tags. This data is intended primarily for use in aviation and as such, sometimes is called airways weather. Note the sharp contrast between Salt Lake City (SLC) and Denver (DEN) weather. A breakdown of Denver's observation follows:

DEN = Denver
WAX = Sky cover
½ = Visibility in miles
S-F = Light snow and fog
035 = Metric barometric pressure
36 = Temperature
31 = Dewpoint
02 = Wind direction 020 degrees

13 = Windspeed in knots
967 = Barometric pressure in inches or altimeter setting

Remaining data is used by pilots and air controllers in evaluating weather restrictions to aircraft operations.

bumpers are multiplied in succeeding bounces. Soon, the trajectory (forecast) varies considerably from what has been envisioned. It is evident that long range forecasts of *specific* weather light the tilt sign.

How, exactly, is a forecast made? Meteorologists gather weather information every hour from all corners of the world. These observations include cloud formation, visibility, barometric readings, temperature, dew point, and wind data. Every three hours, more thorough information accompanies these "obs". A majority of airports in the United States retain trained personnel from the National Weather Service, Federal Aviation Administration, and airlines to accomplish this task. Fire towers, universities, Coast Guard stations, military bases, and ships at sea also contribute observations every hour, three hours, or six hours (Figure A-1).

Much of this information is transmitted to giant computers near Washington, D.C., where it is aggregated, collated, and run through various formulas defining atmospheric motion. The computers then put out weather maps giving the most current state of the atmosphere. These data also become fodder for the equations which attempt to describe current and future trends in the atmosphere. At 12-hour intervals, more data is added as more widely spaced weather stations gather a vertical profile via balloon borne radiosondes. Ascending to measure winds, pressure, humidity, and temperature of the air, radiosondes complete a three-dimensional picture of the weather.

Oceanic areas are data-sparse, while populated land areas have more observation stations yielding more weather information. In the past, this was a problem with regard to hurricanes; unless a ship happened to report a nearby tropical storm, nobody would have known the storm was there. Extrapolation from land-based data often gave a clue, but it also revealed the rich imagination of those doing the extrapolation. Today, satellites immediately confirm what is and is not reality.

At first, satellites pictured only cloud forms — nice for television weather programs and for those who contended that forecasts should be much more accurate. Now, more versatile satellites are not only instant cameras in the sky, but also provide penetrating glimpses of the atmosphere, analyzing temperature and moisture content at various levels. They chart the ocean surface temperature far below, helping to fill the gaps that were once extensive.

There is plenty of information available for people who wish to know or forecast the weather. It clanks across teletypes, rolls out of weather map facsimile machines, and, more recently, spurts from computer terminals linked to the giant computers near the Capitol.

Modern broadcast facilities, private weather forecasting companies, and the National Weather Service are but a few of the users of this readily available data. Computer terminal in hand, a meteorologist (or you) can tap into an hourly source of the latest weather information, avoiding delay in dissemination of important weather facts. This information can be crucial to people who need to protect energy generating devices in their homes.

You also may need information concerning past weather — climatological records. One of the best sources of this kind of weather information can be found in Asheville, North Carolina. The National Climatic Center also is linked to the computers, and can provide various printouts (see sample material from the *Selective Guide to Climatic Data Sources* which follow this discussion) describing past weather at numerous locations across the country. The staff is most helpful and can help you locate, for a nominal fee, any data which may help you in your study of potential energy sites. Contact the Center at:

National Climatic Center
Federal Building
Asheville, NC 28801
(704) 258-2850

Other sources of assistance are:

The Department of Energy
National Energy Information Center
1F-048, 1000 Independence Ave, S.W.
Washington, D.C. 20585

Office of Technology Assessment
Energy Program
U.S. Congress
Washington, D.C. 20510

Solar Energy Research Institute
1617 Cole Blvd.
Golden, Colorado 80401

INTRODUCTION

This GUIDE is designed to assist potential users of climatological data by informing them of the availability of such data in published and unpublished form. It is arranged to indicate the publication(s) in which these data in their various climatological categories (temperature, precipitation, wind, atmospheric pressure, humidity, etc.), both surface and upper air, may be found. A brief review of the pertinent historical facts associated with each publication is given where appropriate. The various climatological tables, charts, and graphs included in each publication are listed, and in many cases abbreviated examples are shown.

Most of the publications described in PART I are available on subscription from the National Climatic Center (NCC). Subscription rates for these publications will be quoted upon request by the Director, National Climatic Center, Federal Building, Asheville, NC 28801. Subscriptions may be entered for a maximum of 3 years at the quoted rate. Copies of back issue publications are also available, but there is a minimum charge of $3.00 per order for shelf-stocked publications, if in print; copies of out-of-print issues can be made for a minimum charge of $5.00 per order (1979 prices). The name and address of the office from which subscriptions or copies of publications that are not distributed by NCC may be obtained are shown where appropriate.

Several climatological atlases haves have been prepared by the National Oceanic and Atmospheric Administration and by agencies in the Department of Defense. The descriptions provide ordering information for these publications.

All back issues of serial climatological publications and many one-time issues containing specialized climatic data have been placed on 4- by 6-in. microfiche. Future issues will also be filmed in order to maintain continuity and integrity in the microfiche file. In addition, some of the unpublished data compilations have been placed on 100-foot reels of 16mm film. Film copies of existing microforms, or paper copies of the publications or data compilations, can be provided as required. Generally, microfilm and microfiche copy costs much less than paper copy. If microforms are desired, contact NCC to determine the availability and cost of the desired materials.

Although this GUIDE refers primarily to published climatological data, it should be noted that a wealth of unpublished climatological data and/or summaries is also available in the NCC files. PART V describes indexes to many of these materials.

Most of the currently published and unpublished materials described in the GUIDE were prepared at NCC from digitized representations (magnetic tape) of the original records. Information about the content and format of these digital data files and how copies of them may be obtained is available from NCC upon request.

Following is a list of the data which can be found in one of these guides.

Part I - Current Serial Publications (issue frequency)

Climatological Data (monthly with annual summary)
Climatological Data for Amundsen-Scott, Antarctica (periodically)
Climatological Data for Arctic Stations (periodically)
Climatological Data, National Summary (monthly with annual summary)
Comparative Climatic Data (annually)
Daily Weather Maps, Weekly Series (weekly)
Environmental/Resource Assessment and Information (weekly)
Global Monitoring of the Environment for Selected Atmospheric Constituents (annually)
High Altitude Meteorological Data (quarterly)
Hourly Precipitation Data (monthly with annual summary)
Local Climatological Data (monthly with annual summary)*
Mariners Weather Log (bimonthly)
Monthly Climatic Data for the World (monthly)
Monthly Summary, Solar Radiation Data (monthly)*
River Forecasts Provided by the National Weather Service (annually)

---

*These sections can be found on the pages following this list.

Snow Cover Surveys (annually)
Storage-Gage Precipitation Data for Western United States (annually)
Storm Data (monthly)
Synoptic Weather Maps, Daily Series, Northern Hemisphere Sea-Level and 500-Millibar Charts and Data Tabulations (monthly)
Weekly Weather and Crop Bulletin (weekly)

Part II — Marine Publications (including atlases)

Marine Climatological Summaries
Mariners Worldwide Climatic Guide to Tropical Storms at Sea
Summary of Synoptic Meteorological Observations, (Area of the World) Coastal Marine Areas
Summary of Synoptic Meteorological Observations for Great Lakes Areas
Tropical Cyclones of the North Atlantic Ocean, 1871-1977
U.S. Navy Marine Climatic Atlas of the World

Part III — Decennial and Intermittent Publications

Climatic Summary of the United States (1930 edition)
Climatic Summary of the United States — Supplement for 1931 through 1952
Climatic Summary of the United States — Supplement for 1951 through 1960 and Unpublished Data Tabulations
Climatography of the United States:
  No. 20 — Climate of (City)
  No. 21 — Climatic Summaries of Resort Areas
  No. 40 — Climate Guide for (Area)
  No. 60 — Climate of (Name of State)
  No. 81 — Monthly Normals of Temperature, Precipitation and Heating and Cooling Degree Days, 1941-70
  No. 82 — Summary of Hourly Observations
  No. 84 — Daily Normals of Temperature and Heating and Cooling Degree Days, 1941-1970 (City)
  No. 85 — Monthly Averages of Temperature and Precipitation for State Climatic Divisions, 1941-1970 (State)
  No. 90 — Airport Climatological Summary
World Weather Records

Part IV — Special Publications (including atlases)

Average Circulation in the Troposphere over the Tropics

Ceiling — Visibility Climatological Study and Systems Enhancement Factors

Climates of the World

Climatic Atlas of the United States*

Engineering Weather Data Manual

Historical Climatology Series

Input Data for Solar Systems*

NOAA Atlas 2: Precipitation Frequency Atlas of the Western United States

NOAA Technical Memorandum NWS HYDRO-35: 5- to 60-Minute Precipitation Frequency for Eastern and Central United States

Selected Climatic Maps of the United States

State, Regional, and National Monthly and Annual Temperatures Weighted by Areas (January 1931-December 1977)

State, Regional, and National Monthly and Annual Total Precipitation Weighted by Area (January 1931-1977)

State, Regional, and National Monthly and Seasonal Cooling Degree Days Weighted by Population (January 1931-December 1977)

State, Regional, and National Monthly and Seasonal Heating

U.S. Air Force Climatic Brief

U.S. Navy Station Climatic Summary

U.S. Weather Bureau Technical Paper No. 40, Rainfall Frequency Atlas of the United States

U.S. Weather Bureau Technical Papers

Worldwide Airfield Summaries

Part V — Data Catalogs and Indexes

FGGE Data Catalogue

GATE Data Catalogue

Guide to Standard Weather Summaries and Climatic Services

Index of Historical Surface Weather Records for (State)

Index of Original Surface Weather Records (Hourly, Synoptic, and Autographic)

Index of Surface Marine Climatic Data Products

Index — Summarized Wind Data

---

*These sections can be found on the pages following this list.

International Field Year of the Great Lakes (IFYGL) Data
  Catalog: United States Archive
SOLMET, Volume 1 — Users Manual, Hourly Solar Radia-
tion — Surface Meteorological Observations
SOLMET, Volume 2 — Final Report, Hourly Solar Radia-
tion — Surface Meteorological Observations
STAR Tabulations Master List

LOCAL CLIMATOLOGICAL DATA

This publication comprises two issues — 1. LOCAL CLIMA-
TOLOGICAL DATA, MONTHLY SUMMARY and 2. LO-
CAL CLIMATOLOGICAL DATA, ANNUAL SUMMARY
WITH COMPARATIVE DATA. Although they are published
individually for about 300 stations, some stations are added
and other stations deleted from time to time. Currently
(1979), they are published individually for those stations
listed on page 35.

LOCAL CLIMATOLOGICAL DATA, MONTHLY SUM-
MARY presents basic climatological data together with a
table of hourly precipitation data for the month on page 1
(Exhibit 43). The second page contains a listing of observations at 3-hour intervals for each day (Exhibit 44).

Predecessor issues were first published as the MONTHLY
METEOROLOGICAL SUMMARY in 1897. In 1948, the
name was changed to MONTHLY CLIMATOLOGICAL
SUMMARY; and in 1952, to its present title. The earlier
issues varied greatly in format and content from station
to station and from time to time. They ranged from a post-
card size single-table issue to a seven-page issue containing
numerous tables of current and comparative data.

A monthly supplement to the LOCAL CLIMATOLOGICAL
DATA was published from 1949 through 1964. It contained
frequency tables, or tables of averages as follows: temperature versus wind speed-relative humidity occurrences (hourly
observations); wind direction versus wind speed occurrences;
hourly and daily occurrences of precipitation amounts;
ceiling-visibility occurrences (hourly observations); occurrences
of weather by hour of day; averages by hours; 24-hour

Exhibit 43

Local Climatological Data

OCTOBER 1979

BOSTON, MASSACHUSETTS

NAT WEATHER SERVICE FCST OFC

GEN LOGAN INTERNATIONAL AP

MONTHLY SUMMARY

OCTOBER 1979   BOSTON, MASSACHUSETTS

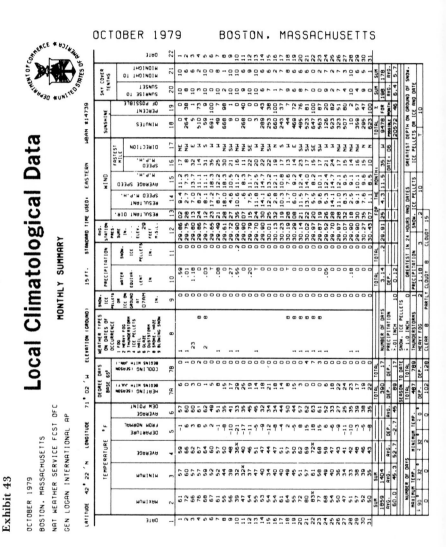

SUMMARY BY HOURS

HOUR LOCAL TIME	SKY COVER TENTHS	STATION PRESSURE IN.	AIR °F	WET BULB °F	DEW PT. °F	RELATIVE HUMIDITY %	WIND SPEED M.P.H.	RESULTANT WIND DIRECTION	RESULTANT WIND SPEED M.P.H.
01	6	29.91	49	47	44	83	10.1	26	5.9
04	5	29.92	48	46	43	84	9.5	27	4.6
07	7	29.94	49	46	44	84	10.2	26	4.7
10	6	29.94	55	51	46	75	12.6	26	5.0
13	7	29.90	57	51	47	70	12.3	24	3.6
16	6	29.88	56	51	46	73	13.4	19	2.3
19	5	29.90	53	49	46	78	11.8	24	5.1
22	4	29.92	50	48	44	81	11.2	26	5.0

* EXTREME FOR THE MONTH - LAST OCCURRENCE IF MORE THAN ONE.
T TRACE AMOUNT
. ALSO ON AN EARLIER DATE, OR DATES.
HEAVY FOG: - VISIBILITY 1/4 MILE OR LESS.
FIGURES FOR WIND DIRECTIONS ARE TENS OF DEGREES CLOCKWISE FROM TRUE NORTH. 00 = CALM.
DATA IN COLS. 6 AND 12-15 ARE BASED ON 7 OR

MORE OBSERVATIONS PER DAY AT 3-HOUR INTERVALS.
FASTEST MILE WIND SPEEDS ARE FASTEST OBSERVED ONE-MINUTE VALUES WHEN DIRECTIONS ARE IN TENS OF DEGREES. THE / WITH THE DIRECTION INDICATES PEAK GUST SPEED.
ANY ERRORS DETECTED WILL BE CORRECTED AND CHANGES IN SUMMARY DATA WILL BE ANNOTATED IN THE ANNUAL SUMMARY.

HOURLY PRECIPITATION (WATER EQUIVALENT IN INCHES)

DAY	A.M. HOUR ENDING AT													P.M. HOUR ENDING AT												
	1	2	3	4	5	6	7	8	9	10	11	12	1	2	3	4	5	6	7	8	9	10	11	12
1	T	T												T				.01	.04	.31				
2	T													T		T				.21			.02	
3																								
4																								
5																.05	1.08							
6	T														.07									
7			.01																					
8				T		T		T					T					T	T					
9																								
10						T	T	.01	T	.02		.02		.01	.05	.01	.05	.09	.04	.04	T			.01
11								.01	.05	.05	.03	.03	T			T		.01	.05	.03	.04	.03		
12																			T					
13														T	T									
14												T						.02	.03	.04	.02	.02		
15																								
16			T																					
17																					T			
18		T																						
19																								
20																								
21																								
22															.04									
23																								
24								T				.01												
25																								
26																								
27																						.01		
28														.01				.03		T	T	.02		
29												T											.01	
30																								
31																								

SUBSCRIPTION PRICE: $3.30 PER YEAR INCLUDING ANNUAL SUMMARY. FOREIGN MAILING $1.95 EXTRA. SINGLE COPY: 25 CENTS FOR MONTHLY ISSUE. 30 CENTS FOR ANNUAL ISSUE. THERE IS A MINIMUM CHARGE OF $3.00 FOR EACH ORDER OF SHELF-STOCKED ISSUES OF PUBLICATIONS. MAKE CHECKS PAYABLE TO DEPARTMENT OF COMMERCE, NOAA. SEND PAYMENTS, ORDERS, AND INQUIRIES TO NATIONAL CLIMATIC CENTER, FEDERAL BUILDING, ASHEVILLE, NORTH CAROLINA 28801.

I CERTIFY THAT THIS IS AN OFFICIAL PUBLICATION OF THE NATIONAL OCEANIC AND ATMOSPHERIC ADMINISTRATION, AND IS COMPILED FROM RECORDS ON FILE AT THE NATIONAL CLIMATIC CENTER, ASHEVILLE, NORTH CAROLINA 28801.

noaa NATIONAL OCEANIC AND ATMOSPHERIC ADMINISTRATION / ENVIRONMENTAL DATA AND INFORMATION SERVICE

DIRECTOR, NATIONAL CLIMATIC CENTER

USCOMM--NOAA--ASHEVILLE   11/26/79   1400

averages; and occurrence of weather by wind direction. It also contained a table showing hourly observations of sky condition, ceiling, visibility, weather, station pressure, temperature, wet bulb temperature, dewpoint, relative humidity, and wind similar to Exhibit 44. The supplement was issued for stations for which 24-hourly observations were available daily. Changes in format were made from time to time. The title from 1949 through 1951 was SPECIAL METEOROLOGICAL SUMMARIES, and from 1952 through 1964 the title was LOCAL CLIMATOLOGICAL DATA, MONTHLY SUPPLEMENT.

The LOCAL CLIMATOLOGICAL DATA, ANNUAL SUMMARY WITH COMPARATIVE DATA was originally issued in 1909 as the ANNUAL METEOROLOGICAL SUMMARY. It was changed to LOCAL CLIMATOLOGICAL SUMMARY in 1949, and in 1952 was changed to LOCAL CLIMATOLOGICAL DATA WITH COMPARATIVE DATA. The words ANNUAL SUMMARY were incorporated in the title in 1966. It contains the following information and data: a narrative climatological summary; a table of meteorological data for the current year (Exhibit 45); a table of normals, means, and extremes covering varying long periods of time (Exhibit 46); and sequential tables of monthly and annual values of average temperature, total precipitation, total snow fall, total heating-degree days, and total cooling-degree days (Exhibit 47). Also included is a Station Location table showing in detail a history of, and related information about, changes in the location and exposure of instruments (Exhibit 48).

Most issues that are 2 or more years old are out of print. All issues have been filmed and can be provided on microfiche or as paper copy prepared from the microfiche.

OBSERVATIONS AT 3-HOUR INTERVALS

Column headings (repeated for each set): HOUR | SKY COVER (TENTHS) | CEILING (HNDS. OF FT.) | VISIBILITY (WHOLE MILES, 16THS MILE) | WEATHER | TEMPERATURE (AIR °F, WET BULB °F, DEW PT. °F) | REL. HUM. % | WIND (DIR, SPEED KNOTS)

NOTES

CEILING
UNL INDICATES UNLIMITED

WEATHER
* TORNADO
T THUNDERSTORM
Q SQUALL
R RAIN
RW RAIN SHOWERS
ZR FREEZING RAIN
L DRIZZLE
ZL FREEZING DRIZZLE
S SNOW
SP SNOW PELLETS
IC ICE CRYSTALS
SW SNOW SHOWERS
SG SNOW GRAINS
IP ICE PELLETS
A HAIL
F FOG
IF ICE FOG
GF GROUND FOG
BD BLOWING DUST
BN BLOWING SAND
BS BLOWING SNOW
BY BLOWING SPRAY
K SMOKE
H HAZE
D DUST

WIND
DIRECTIONS ARE THOSE FROM WHICH THE WIND BLOWS, INDICATED IN TENS OF DEGREES FROM TRUE NORTH: I.E., 09 FOR EAST, 18 FOR SOUTH, 27 FOR WEST. ENTRY OF 00 IN THE DIRECTION COLUMN INDICATES CALM.

SPEED IS EXPRESSED IN KNOTS; MULTIPLY BY 1.15 TO CONVERT TO MILES PER HOUR.

Sample of Exhibit 44

Annual Summary With Comparative Data

Climate is the composite of numerous weather elements. Three important influences are responsible for the main features of Boston's climate. First, the latitude (42° N) places the city in the zone of prevailing west to east atmospheric flow in which are encompassed the northward and southward movements of large bodies of air from tropical and polar regions. This results in variety and changeability of the weather elements. Secondly, Boston is situated on or near several tracks frequently followed by systems of low air pressure. The consequent fluctuations from fair to cloudy or stormy conditions reinforce the influence of the first factor, while also assuring a rather dependable precipitation supply. The third factor, Boston's east-coast location, is a moderating factor affecting temperature extremes of winter and summer.

Hot summer afternoons are frequently relieved by the locally celebrated "sea-breeze," as air flows inland from the cool water surface to displace the warm westerly current. This refreshing east wind is more commonly experienced along the shore than in the interior of the city or the western suburbs. In winter, under appropriate conditions, the severity of cold waves is reduced by the nearness of the then relatively warm water. The average date of the last occurrence of freezing temperature in spring is April 8; the latest is May 3, 1874 and 1882. The average date of the first occurrence of freezing temperature in autumn is November 7; the earliest on record is October 5, 1881. In suburban areas, especially away from the coast, these dates are later in spring and earlier in autumn by up to one month in the more susceptible localities.

Boston has no dry season. For most years the longest run of days with no measurable precipitation does not extend much more than two weeks. This may occur at any time of year. Most growing seasons have several shorter dry spells during which irrigation for high-value crops may be useful.

Much of the rainfall from June to September comes from showers and thunderstorms. During the rest of the year, low pressure systems pass more or less regularly and produce precipitation on an average of roughly one day in three. Coastal storms, or "northeasters," are prolific producers of rain and snow. The main snow season extends from December through March. The average number of days with four inches or more of snowfall is four per season, and days with seven inches or more come about twice per season. Periods when the ground is bare or nearly bare of snow may occur at any time in the winter.

Relative humidity has been known to fall as low as 5% (May 10, 1962), but such desert dryness is very rare. Heavy fog occurs on an average of about two days per month with its prevalence increasing eastward from the interior of Boston Bay to the open water beyond.

The greatest number of hours of sunshine recorded in any month was 390, or 86% of possible, in June 1912, while the least was 60 hours, or 21%, in December 1972.

Although winds of 32 m.p.h. or higher may be expected on at least one day in every month of the year, gales are both more common and more severe in winter.

Exhibit 45 Meteorological Data for the Current Year

Station: BOSTON, MASSACHUSETTS #14739   GEN LOGAN INTERNATIONAL AP   Standard time used: EASTERN

Month	Temperature °F Averages Daily maximum	Daily minimum	Monthly	Extremes Highest	Date	Lowest	Date	Degree days Base 65°F Heating	Cooling	Precipitation in inches Water equivalent Total	Greatest in 24 hrs.	Date	Snow, Ice pellets Total	Greatest in 24 hrs.	Date	Relative humidity, pct. Hour 01	Hour 07	Hour 13	Hour 19
JAN	39.1	25.8	32.5	61	2	4	19	1002	0	10.55	2.72	20-21	10.5	4.2	17	74	74	66	71
FEB	30.4	15.8	23.1	53	28	-3	11	1169	0	3.46	1.77	25-26	6.6	3.7	7-8	54	56	45	49
MAR	49.9	35.0	42.5	72	23	19	16	691	0	3.03	1.19	6-7	T	T	19	70	71	62	68
APR	55.6	41.7	48.7	77	24	33	8	481	0	3.19	1.19	27-28	0.4	0.3	9	72	71	61	64
MAY	68.5	53.7	61.1	95	9	45	2	149	35	4.24	1.28	23-24	0.0	0.0		78	75	65	70
JUN	77.3	59.1	68.2	95	16	50	13	19	122	0.86	0.32	11-12	0.0	0.0		78	73	55	67
JUL	82.9	66.1	74.5	94	13	55	5	2	304	2.36	0.94	18	0.0	0.0		84	80	63	73
AUG	78.6	64.7	71.7	91	2	54	13	15	226	5.02	1.88	12-13	0.0	0.0		84	83	68	75
SEP	72.8	57.0	64.9	85	3	42	20	80	85	3.61	1.73	21-22	0.0	0.0		80	82	65	73
OCT	60.0	45.3	52.7	83	22	32	11	390	17	3.14	1.18	3	0.2	0.2	10	83	84	70	78
NOV	55.9	41.2	48.6	72	2	29	30	484	0	3.29	1.44	2-3	T	T	16	79	83	63	74
DEC	44.2	29.1	36.7	68	12	5	19	873	0	1.42	0.49	13	2.0	1.5	13	65	67	53	60
YEAR	59.6	44.5	52.1	95	JUN 16	-3	FEB 11	5355	789	44.17	2.72	JAN 20-21	19.7	4.2	JAN 17	75	75	61	69

Latitude: 42° 22' N   Longitude: 71° 02' W   Elevation (ground): 15 feet   Year: 1979

Wind Resultant Direction	Speed m.p.h.	Average speed m.p.h.	Fastest mile Speed m.p.h.	Direction	Date	Percent of possible sunshine	Average sky cover, tenths, sunrise to sunset	Number of days Sunrise to sunset Clear	Partly cloudy	Cloudy	Precipitation .01 inch or more	Snow, Ice pellets 1.0 inch or more	Thunderstorms	Heavy fog, visibility ¼ mile or less	Temperature °F Maximum 90° and above	(b) 32° and below	Minimum 32° and below	0° and below	Average station pressure mb Elev. 29 feet m.s.l.
29	6.8	15.0	45	E	25	40	7.1	8	1	22	18	4	1	2	0	11	21	0	1011.2
31	11.7	15.8	34	NW	6	64	4.8	14	4	10	9	2	0	1	0	16	25	6	1016.6
26	2.1	13.0	31	S	24	49	7.0	6	8	17	12	0	1	3	0	0	11	0	1017.3
35	1.3	13.0	36	NW	10	49	7.1	8	3	19	13	0	1	3	0	0	0	0	1014.6
35	0.9	11.4	25	NW	5	55	6.8	7	8	16	16	0	1	6	2	0	0	0	1015.2
22	4.6	12.1	29	NW	12	75	4.7	9	15	6	6	0	2	0	4	0	0	0	1016.6
20	3.3	10.7	40	W	2	67	5.5	8	16	7	8	0	3	5	3	0	0	0	1014.6
22	2.8	11.3	30	SW	10	50	6.7	5	13	13	14	0	7	3	3	0	0	0	1014.9
24	3.3	11.2	40	S	6	64	5.6	9	12	9	7	0	2	1	0	0	0	0	1016.6
25	4.3	11.5	35	W	6	46	6.4	8	8	15	10	0	1	2	0	0	2	0	1012.9
26	5.1	11.7	43	S	26	52	6.5	9	3	18	10	0	0	4	0	0	3	0	1017.6
28	7.6	13.6	42	W	8	58	5.3	12	8	11	8	1	0	3	0	3	18	0	1015.9
27	3.6	12.5	45	E	JAN 25	56	6.1	103	99	163	131	7	19	33	12	30	80	6	1015.3

Exhibit 46   Normals, Means, and Extremes

Month	Temperatures °F							Normal Degree days Base 65 °F		Precipitation in inches									
	Normal			Extremes						Water equivalent							Snow, Ice pellets		
	Daily maximum	Daily minimum	Monthly	Record highest	Year	Record lowest	Year	Heating	Cooling	Normal	Maximum monthly	Year	Minimum monthly	Year	Maximum in 24 hrs.	Year	Maximum monthly	Year	Maximum in 24 hrs.	Year
(a)				28		28					28			28			44		44	
J	35.9	22.5	29.2	63	1974	-12	1957	1110	0	3.69	10.55	1979	0.89	1970	2.72	1979	35.9	1978	21.0	1978
F	37.5	23.3	30.4	68	1957	-4	1961	969	0	3.54	7.08	1969	1.15	1968	2.68	1969	41.3	1969	23.6	1978
M	44.6	31.5	38.1	81	1977	6	1967	834	0	4.01	11.00	1953	1.48	1962	4.13	1968	31.2	1956	17.7	1960
A	56.3	40.8	48.6	94	1976	17	1954	492	0	3.49	7.82	1958	1.24	1966	2.31	1973	3.3	1967	3.1	1956
M	67.1	50.1	58.6	95	1979	34	1956	218	20	3.47	13.38	1954	0.53	1964	5.74	1954	0.5	1977	0.5	1977
J	76.6	59.3	68.0	100	1952	46	1965	27	117	3.19	8.63	1959	0.48	1953	2.46	1960	0.0		0.0	
J	81.4	65.1	73.3	102	1977	54	1965	0	260	2.74	8.12	1959	0.52	1952	2.42	1959	0.0		0.0	
A	79.3	63.3	71.3	102	1975	47	1965	8	203	3.46	17.09	1955	0.83	1972	8.40	1955	0.0		0.0	
S	72.2	56.7	64.5	100	1953	38	1965	76	61	3.16	8.31	1954	0.35	1957	5.64	1954	0.0		0.0	
O	63.2	47.5	55.4	90	1963	28	1976	301	0	3.02	8.68	1962	0.96	1967	4.26	1962	0.2	1979	0.2	1979
N	51.7	38.7	45.2	77	1974	17	1978	594	0	4.51	8.18	1969	0.64	1976	3.33	1955	10.0	1938	8.0	1940
D	39.3	26.6	33.0	70	1966	-4	1962	992	0	4.24	9.74	1969	1.03	1955	4.17	1969	27.9	1970	13.0	1960
YR	58.7	43.8	51.3	102	JUL 1977	-12	JAN 1957	5621	661	42.52	17.09	1955	0.35	SEP 1957	8.40	AUG 1955	41.3	FEB 1969	23.6	FEB 1978

(a) Length of record, years, through the current year unless otherwise noted, based on January data.
(b) 70° and above at Alaskan stations.
* Less than one half.
T Trace.

NORMALS - Based on record for the 1941-1970 period.
DATE OF AN EXTREME - The most recent in cases of multiple occurrence.
PREVAILING WIND DIRECTION - Record through 1963.
WIND DIRECTION - Numerals indicate tens of degrees clockwise from true north. 00 indicates calm.
FASTEST MILE WIND - Speed is fastest observed 1-minute value when the direction is in tens of degrees.

Exhibit 47

Average Temperature

Year	Jan	Feb	Mar	Apr	May	June	July	Aug	Sept	Oct	Nov	Dec	Annual
1940	23.0	29.6	33.1	43.6	56.2	65.1	71.6	68.4	63.3	50.6	42.9	34.3	48.5
1941	25.2	29.4	33.4	51.6	59.8	68.2	71.4	70.6	66.0	55.9	48.0	35.2	51.2
1942	28.6	27.0	40.8	49.7	60.8	67.4	71.1	70.7	64.5	55.8	43.5	28.6	50.7
1943	25.5	30.6	36.0	43.4	57.6	71.2	74.1	71.0	63.0	53.8	43.3	29.6	49.9
1944	31.0	29.6	34.1	44.6	63.2	67.0	73.8	74.7	65.0	53.8	43.2	30.8	50.9
1945	23.8	30.5	46.3	52.5	55.2	66.6	71.9	70.8	67.1	53.1	45.5	28.5	51.0
1976	26.1	37.3	41.2	55.1	60.2	73.4	72.9	72.0	64.9	52.3	41.9	29.0	52.2
1977	23.3	30.7	44.7	51.3	62.6	67.4	74.9	73.4	64.4	55.3	48.1	34.2	52.5
1978	28.5	27.1	36.2	48.8	59.3	68.3	72.1	71.6	61.4	52.5	43.6	35.3	50.4
1979	32.5	23.1	42.5	48.7	61.1	68.2	74.5	71.7	64.9	52.7	48.6	36.7	52.1
RECORD													
MEAN	28.8	29.1	37.0	47.1	57.8	67.1	72.6	70.8	64.0	54.1	43.5	32.7	50.4
MAX	36.3	36.8	44.5	55.1	66.4	75.8	81.0	78.8	72.0	62.0	50.6	39.7	58.3
MIN	21.3	21.4	29.5	39.0	49.2	58.3	64.2	62.7	56.0	46.1	36.4	25.6	42.5

Precipitation

Year	Jan	Feb	Mar	Apr	May	June	July	Aug	Sept	Oct	Nov	Dec	Annual
1940	1.68	4.78	3.83	4.58	3.28	1.80	3.17	0.85	2.32	0.76	6.24	2.76	36.05
1976	5.29	2.45	2.42	2.00	1.98	0.58	4.30	7.99	1.56	4.16	0.64	3.35	36.72
1977	4.41	2.40	4.76	4.07	3.52	2.49	2.21	2.91	4.03	4.63	2.54	6.20	44.17
1978	8.12	2.87	2.46	1.79	4.50	1.53	1.48	4.62	1.30	3.13	2.21	3.63	37.64
1979	10.55	3.46	3.03	3.19	4.24	0.86	2.36	5.02	3.61	3.14	3.29	1.42	44.17
RECORD MEAN	3.71	3.38	3.82	3.54	3.26	3.10	3.13	3.63	3.23	3.24	3.83	3.67	41.54

Relative humidity pct.				Wind					Pct. of possible sunshine	Mean sky cover, tenths, sunrise to sunset	Mean number of days												Average station pressure mb.
						Fastest mile					Sunrise to sunset			Precipitation .01 inch or more	Snow, Ice pellets 1.0 inch or more	Thunderstorms	Heavy fog, visibility ¼ mile or less	Temperatures °F Max.		Min.			
Hour 01	Hour 07	Hour 13	Hour 19	Mean speed m.p.h.	Prevailing direction	Speed m.p.h.	Direction	Year			Clear	Partly cloudy	Cloudy					90° and above (b)	32° and below	32° and below	0° and below		Elev. 29 feet m.s.l.
(Local time)																							7
15	15	15	15	22	15	21	21		44	44	44	44	44	28	44	44	44	15	15	15	15		15
66	68	58	62	14.2	NW	61	NW	1974	53	6.2	9	7	15	12	3	*	2	0	12	25	1		1014.0
64	66	56	59	14.1	WNW	61	NE	1978	57	6.1	8	7	13	11	3	*	2	0	9	24	1		1014.3
67	68	57	62	13.9	NW	60	NE	1977	57	6.4	8	8	15	12	2	1	2	0	2	17	0		1014.5
66	66	53	59	13.3	WNW	52	NW	1963	57	6.4	7	9	14	11	*	1	2	*	0	3	0		1012.6
73	71	58	64	12.2	SW	50	NE	1967	59	6.5	6	11	14	12	0	2	3	*	0	0	0		1013.7
78	74	59	67	11.4	SW	40	NW	1959	64	6.2	7	10	13	10	0	4	2	3	0	0	0		1014.5
77	73	56	66	10.8	SW	46	N	1977	66	6.1	7	12	12	9	0	4	2	5	0	0	0		1013.9
79	76	59	69	10.7	SW	45	SW	1971	66	5.7	9	11	11	10	0	4	2	3	0	0	0		1016.2
80	79	61	72	11.2	SW	57	S	1960	64	5.5	10	9	11	9	0	2	2	1	0	0	0		1016.5
75	76	58	68	12.1	SW	45	NW	1963	61	5.5	11	8	12	9	0	1	2	0	0	1	0		1016.4
72	75	61	68	12.9	SW	54	NE	1968	51	6.4	8	7	15	11	*	*	2	0	*	6	0		1016.1
69	71	60	65	13.8	WNW	49	NW	1962	53	6.2	9	7	15	12	2	*	1	0	5	21	*		1015.1
72	72	58	65	12.6	SW	61	NE	FEB 1978	60	6.1	99	106	160	128	11	19	23	12	28	98	1		1014.8

Heating Degree Days

BOSTON, MA

Season	July	Aug	Sept	Oct	Nov	Dec	Jan	Feb	Mar	Apr	May	June	Total
1959-60	1	7	79	319	611	885	1048	855	992	493	166	33	5489
1975-76	0	8	70	239	395	941	1198	800	733	331	166	16	4897
1976-77	1	10	55	393	688	1108	1290	956	623	414	158	43	5739
1977-78	0	4	85	304	498	948	1127	1057	885	480	209	18	5615
1978-79	11	11	150	381	635	916	1002	1169	691	481	149	19	5615
1979-80	2	15	80	390	484	873							

Cooling Degree Days

Year	Jan	Feb	Mar	Apr	May	June	July	Aug	Sept	Oct	Nov	Dec	Total
1969	0	0	0	9	13	156	196	297	74	1	0	0	746
1970	0	0	0	0	25	118	294	273	91	9	0	0	810
1976	0	0	0	43	25	276	251	231	61	8	0	0	895
1977	0	0	1	13	92	124	314	272	75	6	0	0	897
1978	0	0	0	0	40	122	237	221	48	0	0	0	668
1979	0	0	0	0	35	122	304	226	85	17	0	0	789

Snowfall

Season	July	Aug	Sept	Oct	Nov	Dec	Jan	Feb	Mar	Apr	May	June	Total
1940-41	0.0	0.0	0.0	T	8.5	4.5	20.4	1.3	13.1	0.0	T	0.0	47.8
1941-42	0.0	0.0	0.0	T	T	0.2	8.2	6.2	7.9	1.5	0.0	0.0	24.0
1975-76	0.0	0.0	0.0	T	0.1	19.3	15.0	1.4	10.8	T	0.0	0.0	46.6
1976-77	0.0	0.0	0.0	0.0	1.0	17.2	23.2	5.9	10.7	T	0.5	0.0	58.5
1977-78	0.0	0.0	0.0	0.0	0.7	5.2	35.9	27.2	16.1	T	0.0	0.0	85.1
1978-79	0.0	0.0	0.0	0.0	4.2	5.8	10.5	6.6	T	0.4	0.0	0.0	27.5
1979-80	0.0	0.0	0.0	0.2	T	2.0							
RECORD MEAN	0.0	0.0	0.0	T	1.2	7.9	12.7	12.0	8.1	0.7	T	0.0	42.6

STATION LOCATION

BOSTON, MASSACHUSETTS

Exhibit 48

Location	Occupied from	Occupied to	Airline distance and direction from previous location	Latitude North	Longitude West	Elevation above Sea level (Ground at temperature site)	Wind instruments	Extreme thermometers	Psychrometer	Sunshine Switch	Tipping bucket rain gage	Weighing rain gage	8" rain gage	Hygrothermometer	Automatic Observing Equipment	Remarks (Type M = AMOS, T = AUTOB)
CITY																
Old State House, corner State & Devonshire Sts.	10/20/70	1/09/71		42° 21'	71° 04'	16										Ground elevation approximate.
103 Court Street	1/10/71	8/12/75	600 ft. NW	42° 21'	71° 04'	40										Ground elevation approximate.
Equitable Building Corner Milk & Devonshire Streets	8/12/75	10/01/84	1200 ft. SE	42° 21'	71° 04'	12	172	156	156				162			
Old U. S. Post ʳ and Courthouͥ 'ilk, Deᵛ	10/01/84	6/07/?ᵇ	˙, NE	42° 21'	˙04'	17	188	115	1˙			154	174 15.			rain gage moved from bad ˙top east tower to ˙˙ ˙t above pˡ
AIRPORT																
U. S. Army Hangar No. 1 Boston Airport East Boston	10/15/26	4/01/27		42° 22'	71° 02'	3										Pibal only.
ⁿection F, Army Base ⁿh Boston	4/01/27	11/01/27	1-3/4 mi. S	42° 21'	71° 02'	2	143									Pibal only.
˙ South of	ⁿ1-3/4 mi. N	42°˙˙	ⁿ° 02'		2?											pⁱˑ ˙˙

MONTHLY SUMMARY, SOLAR RADIATION DATA

This publication, issued monthly only, began with data for January 1977. It presents for stations in the National Oceanic and Atmospheric Administration network (Exhibit 52) edited hourly and daily values of global (hemispheric) solar radiation in kilojoules per square meter (Exhibit 53). Data which are estimated, obtained from radiation models, or judged to be questionable are flagged. A station index which shows the type(s) of data published for each station (Exhibit 54) and descriptions of the data processing and flagging procedures are also included in each issue. The number of stations in the observing network is expected to increase in the 1980s. Normal incidence diffuse, and other types of solar radiation data will be included in this monthly publication in future years.

Solar radiation data for earlier years have been published in several publications. Data for as many as 33 stations that reported daily global and/or normal incidence radiation were published in the March 1914 through December 1949 issues of the MONTHLY WEATHER REVIEW. Daily global solar radiation data for as many as 80 stations were published in CLIMATOLOGICAL DATA, NATIONAL SUMMARY (CDNS) from January 1950 through August 1972 and from July 1975 through December 1976. Normal incidence solar radiation and net radiation data have been published in CDNS for a few stations since January 1950 (Exhibit 25). Monthly and annual means of daily global solar radiation data for the current year and the period of record for 62 National Weather Service stations were published in the annual issues of LOCAL CLIMATOLOGICAL DATA from 1963 through 1971. Much of the published global solar radiation data prior to July 1975 are considered questionable and should be used with caution.

CLIMATIC ATLAS OF THE UNITED STATES

This Atlas was published in June 1968. It depicts the climate of the United States in terms of the distribution and variation of constituent climatic elements.

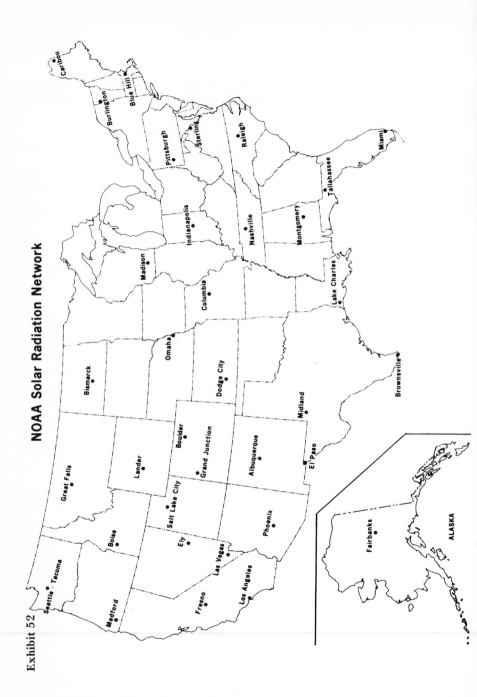

Exhibit 52

NOAA Solar Radiation Network

Exhibit 53

PHOENIX, AZ
NOVEMBER 1977

STATION 23183
N33.26 W112.01 ELEV (M MSL) 0339
PYRANOMETER SPEC SR-75

EDITED GLOBAL RADIATION
RADIATION FOR EACH HOUR ENDING AT LOCAL STANDARD TIME (KILOJOULES PER SQUARE METER)

Hours 1–6 and 19–24 are 0 for every day (except hour 7, which is 4 on days 03 and 04). The readable data is tabulated below.

DAY	7	8	9	10	11	12	13	14	15	16	17	18	TOTAL
01	0	234	727	1559	2178	2160	2080	2300	1876	1249	544	47	15686
02	0	331	997	1660	2167	2236	2216	2236	1786	1177	482	40	15751
03	4	310	979	1616	2161	2228	2204	2228	1818	1213	526	36	15610
04	4	281	918	1523	2004	2081	2002	1591	785	799	497	43	12521
05	0	234	907	1516	2071	2189	2189	2189	1757	1163	472	32	14963
06	0	32	155	447	1041	1192	1055	1055	544	284	76	0	7651
07	0	342	814	1391	868	1192	1876	1192	655	576	367	36	10055
08	0	256	900	1530	2322	2081	2081	2081	1642	1080	450	32	14444
09	0	256	925	1571	2426	2243	2243	2243	1811	1206	497	36	15416
10	0	252	896	1584	2437	2236	2243	2236	1836	1202	493	36	15451
11	0	50	817	1465	2185	2185	2185	2185	1739	1163	450	29	14622
12	0	137	472	1163	2135	2135	2135	2135	1714	1105	450	22	13606
13	0	227	857	1490	2185	2185	2185	2185	1472	936	353	18	14141
14	0	148	911	1422	2027	2027	2027	2027	1624	1033	418	18	13898
15	0	130	554	1145	1871	1843	1843	1843	1688	947	367	18	12834
16	0	176	778	1390	1872	1398	1398	1398	1598	1022	392	14	13592
17	0	180	778	1390	1876	1938	1938	1938	1631	1055	403	14	13772
18	0	166	785	727	792	2002	2002	2002	1598	1087	403	14	10695
19	0	22	346	1105	1656	2009	2009	2009	1598	943	385	22	12525
20	0	151	626	1303	1071	1915	1915	1915	1166	803	421	32	11130
21	0	173	727	1321	1552	1552	1552	1552	745	724	371	14	10170
22	0	184	716	1350	1501	1501	1501	1501	1177	637	266	11	11340
23	0	140	724	1320	2113	1951	1951	1951	1537	954	349	11	13006
24	0	68	630	1280	2081	1922	1922	1922	1530	976	342	11	12600
25	0	133	684	1280	2088	1915	1915	1915	1530	968	335	7	12743
26	0	144	648	1250	2146	1955	1955	1955	1552	958	364	11	12918
27	0	101	630	1240	1890	1724	1724	1724	1246	572	223	4	11397
28	0	97	634	1220	2034	1908	1908	1908	1480	850	274	11	12180
29	0	115	659	1271	1960	1904	1904	1904	1321	1321	331	14	12621
30	0	97	587	1195	1802	1847	1847	1847	1534	947	223	4	12006
MEAN	0	172	726	1327	1917	1929	1955	1929	1466	955	384	21	12978

The climatic maps of the United States present in uniform
format a series of analyses showing the national distribution
of monthly and annual mean, normal and/or extreme values
of temperature, precipitation, wind, barometric pressure,
relative humidity, dewpoint, sunshine, sky cover, heating-
degree days, solar radiation, and evaporation.

The individual analyses were originally prepared as separate
sheets. The entire set — a total of 40 large sheets (16" x
21½") containing 271 climatic maps and 15 tables — has
been collected and bound into this comprehensive atlas.
Individual sheets are still available as separates.

The following analyses or sheets are contained in the atlas:

Normal Daily Maximum, Minimum, Average, Range and Ex-
 tremes of Temperature (°F), Monthly
Mean Number of Days Maximum Temperature 90°F and
 Above, Monthly and Annual
Mean Number of Days Minimum Temperature 32°F and
 Below, Monthly and Annual
Mean Date of Last 32°F Temperature in Spring
Mean Date of First 32°F Temperature in Autumn
Mean Length of Freeze-Free Period (Days)
Mean Length of Period Between Specified Temperature
 Limits and Freeze Free Period, Annual
Normal Total Heating Degree Days, Monthly and Annual
Normal Total Precipitation (Inches), Monthly and Annual
Mean Total Precipitation (Inches), by State Climatic Division,
 Monthly and Annual
State Climatic Divisions
Mean Annual Precipitation in Millions of Gallons of Water
 Per Square Mile by State Climatic Divisions
Mean Annual Precipitation in Millions of Gallons of Water
 Per Capita by State Climatic Divisions
Mean Total Snowfall (Inches)
Mean Monthly Total Snowfall (Inches), for Selected Stations
Mean Number of Days with 0.01 Inch or More of Precipita-
 tion, Monthly and Annual
Mean Dewpoint Temperature (°F), Monthly and Annual
Maximum Persisting 12-Hour 1000-mb Dewpoint Tempera-
 ture (°F), Monthly and of Record
Mean Relative Humidity (%), Monthly and Annual

Mean Pan and Lake Evaporation
Mean Percentage of Possible Sunshine, Monthly and Annual
Mean Total Hours of Sunshine, Monthly and Annual
Mean Daily Solar Radiation, Monthly and Annual*
Mean Sky Cover, Sunrise to Sunset, Monthly and Annual
Prevailing Direction, Mean Speed (M.P.H.), and Fastest Mile
    of Wind, Monthly and Annual
Surface Wind Roses, Monthly and Annual; Resultant Surface
    Winds, Midseasonal
Normal Sea-Level Pressures, Monthly and Annual

INPUT DATA FOR SOLAR SYSTEMS

This special report was prepared in 1978 by the National
Oceanic and Atmospheric Administration, Environmental
Data and Information Service, National Climatic Center for
the U.S. Department of Energy, Division of Solar Technology. The tables (Exhibit 127) presented in this report are
by-products of efforts to provide taped meteorological and
solar radiation data as inputs to requester's energy design
and performance programs. Tabular values are climatological
means for 248 U.S. stations.

The monthly and annual normals of maximum, minimum,
and average temperatures, and of heating — and cooling —
degree days, were extracted from CLIMATOGRAPHY OF
THE UNITED STATES NO. 81 (BY STATE) and the 1977
issues of LOCAL CLIMATOLOGICAL DATA, ANNUAL
SUMMARY WITH COMPARATIVE DATA. Zeros that
appear for all values in a normals column indicate that the
1941 through 1970 period normals were not available for the
station. A total of 43 stations have at least two normals
columns filled with zeros and 16 have no normals data at all.

Average daily values of total hemispheric (global) solar radiation on a horizontal surface were based on corrected (rehabilitated) hourly measurements for 26 stations and derived
values from the corrected measurements for the remaining
222 stations. The 26 rehabilitated data stations are identified.

---

*Data upon which these charts are based are questionable; charts should
  be used with caution.

Exhibit 127

```
********************************************************
          STATION: CHARLOTTE            STATE: NC
          --------------------          --------
STATION NUMBER: 13881  LATITUDE: 3513N  LONGITUDE: 8056W  ELEVATION: 234
```

MONTH	NORMAL TEMPERATURE (DEG F)*			NORMAL DEGREE DAYS* BASE 65 DEG F		TOTAL HEMISPHERIC MEAN DAILY SOLAR RADIATION#		
	DAILY MAXIMUM	DAILY MINIMUM	MONTHLY	HEATING	COOLING	BTU/FT2	KJ/M2	LANGLEYS
JAN	52.1	32.1	42.1	710	0	719.0	8160.0	195.0
FEB	54.9	33.1	44.0	588	0	971.0	11020.0	263.4
MAR	62.2	39.0	50.6	461	15	1317.5	14952.0	357.4
APR	72.7	48.9	60.8	145	19	1695.0	19236.0	459.8
MAY	80.2	57.4	68.8	34	152	1855.6	21059.0	503.3
JUN	86.4	65.3	75.9	0	327	1921.1	21802.0	521.1
JUL	88.3	68.7	78.5	0	419	1830.9	20779.0	496.6
AUG	87.4	67.9	77.7	0	394	1695.0	19236.0	459.8
SEP	82.0	61.9	72.0	10	220	1415.6	16065.0	384.0
OCT	73.1	50.3	61.7	152	50	1173.4	13317.0	318.3
NOV	62.4	39.6	51.0	420	0	865.5	9823.0	234.8
DEC	52.5	32.4	42.5	698	0	672.4	7631.0	182.4
ANN	71.2	49.7	60.5	3218	1596	1344.4	15257.0	364.7

* BASED ON 1941-1970 PERIOD   # AS NOTED IN SOLMET VOLUME 1

```
********************************************************
********************************************************
```

Most of the average values are based on a 24-25 year period. SOLMET MANUALS VOLUME 1 USER'S MANUAL and VOLUME 2 — FINAL REPORT list the exact period as well as providing information on the rehabilitation of hourly solar radiation data. Average daily values for 14 stations were computed from a composite period of record where the station occupied two different nearby locations. For all cases, tables list the station name, number, and coordinates of the last location.

Appendix B

HEAT
PUMPS

Since heat pumps depend upon favorable air temperatures, they are somewhat weather and climate related; and because use of heat pumps is increasing, we wanted to say a few words about them in this book. Heat pumps provide heat during cold season and reverse providing air conditioning during warm season, making them especially valuable in climates requiring both. System selection, of course, depends upon both applications, and must take into account the disadvantages of heat pumps in colder climes.

Heat pumps are fueled by electricity. In fact, they simply use electricity more efficiently in producing heat than commonplace electrical resistance or strip heating. In the latter, as in a toaster, one cent's worth of electricity provides one cent's worth of heat as determined by the glowing material. A heat pump takes the same amount of electricity and utilizes it to "steal" heat from ambient outside air. For instance, were the outside temperature standing at 50°F,

204

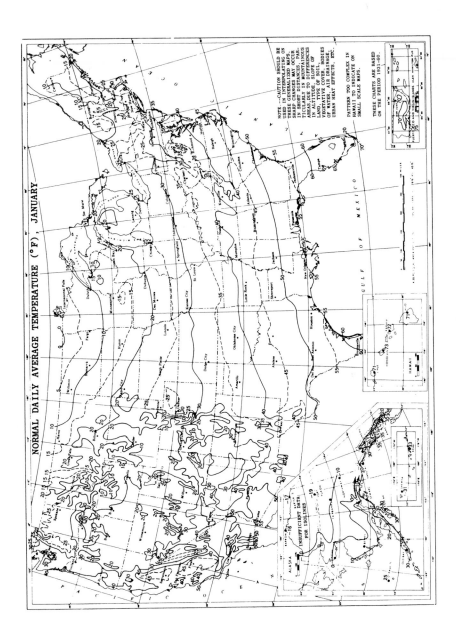

NORMAL DAILY AVERAGE TEMPERATURE (°F), JANUARY

the mechanism might steal 20° from the air and return it to the outdoors at 30°. Continuously acquiring heat, the system injects the gain into a dwelling. At 40° F, a heat pump could provide roughly three cents' worth of heat for every cent of electricity it uses. It does even better at 50°.

Sounds great — to a certain degree. As outside temperature falls, the system must work harder to effect a gain, requiring more fuel (electricity). Between 30 and 35° F, diminished efficiency and increased home heating demand combine to reduce the pump's effectiveness. Indeed, at lower temperatures, it takes as much electricity to acquire heat with the pump as it would to electrify a conventional resistance heater.

In considering heat pumps, then, you need to know how often temperature equals or falls below this threshold. Regions which experience prolonged cold are not optimum heat pump locales. Climatic records should be examined for the average temperature over a period of time. For example, during January use of a heat pump makes little sense over much of the northern half of the United States (refer to the map below). Average temperature summaries during heating season also would help in making a decision. Of course, other considerations apply: most notably, the desire for air conditioning during warm season. Heat pumps utilizing other sources of heat — solar assisted and ground water heat pumps are two examples — should be examined as well.

Appendix C

USEFUL ENERGY FACTS

Energy is an abstract entity, often defined as the ability to do work. Energy makes things happen.

In this book we use two measures of energy, those most commonly used in the United States: the Btu (British thermal unit) and the kilowatt hour. The Btu usually refers to heat energy; the kilowatt hour is commonly applied to electrical energy. The two are uniquely related — one kilowatt-hour equals 3412 Btu's — so one term would suffice, but the above usage is conventional. Other terms of measure you may run across in your reading are included at the end of this appendix.

Power is the *rate* at which energy is used, dissipated, applied, or converted: Btu's per hour, for example, in the case of thermal energy; kilowatt hours per hour, or simply kilowatts, in the case of electrical energy. Power and energy often are confused, but they shouldn't be. Just as speed (miles per hour)

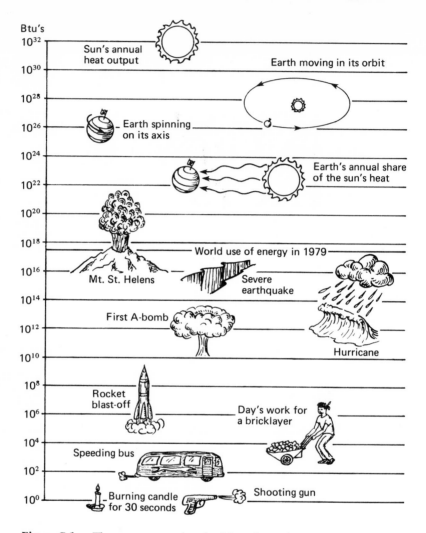

Figure C-1   The energy associated with various phenomena.

is the *rate* at which distance (miles) is covered, power is the *rate* at which energy is used. The confusion may stem from the fact that the term kilowatt, a unit of power, doesn't explicitly mention time.

You commonly pay for energy, not power: the energy in a gallon of gasoline, a kilowatt hour of electricity, or a cord of wood, for example. But the electrical generating capacity of the United States is the rate at which energy could be produced, the *power* in megawatts, if every generator were turned on.

In dealing with the energy in atmospheric phenomena, we are dealing with large quantities. Since the units used for measuring energy are relatively small quantities, we must use a lot of these small units to describe meteorological energies. Here are the common prefixes for these large numbers and a few tidbits of energy information:

one million = one thousand thousand (mega)

one billion = one thousand million (giga)

one trillion = one million million (tera)

one quadrillion = one thousand million million

A quadrillion Btu's is called simply a "quad" or "Q" for short.

1 kilowatt hour is equivalent to 3412 Btu of energy.

1 kilowatt (one thousand watts) is power produced at the rate of 3412 Btu's per hour (in the form of heat), or one kilowatt hour per hour (usually applied to electricity).

1 megawatt is equal to one million watts, or one thousand kilowatts.

The world's use of energy in 1979 was 297 quadrillion Btu's (297 quads).

The use of energy in the United States totaled 78 quads in 1980.

Each American uses energy equivalent to a barrel of oil every six days.

The United States paid more than $60 billion in 1979 for imported oil, and $80 billion in 1980 in spite of a 20 percent reduction in imports.

The electrical generating capacity of the United States in 1979 was approximately 500,000 megawatts, or 500 gigawatts.

The proven reserves of various fossil energy sources in the
United States and in the world are as follows:

	United States	*World*
Oil	157Q	3721Q
Coal	4577	16,482
Gas	201	2653

Conversion Table: Energy and Power Equivalents

1 watt (w) = 1 joule (j) for 1 second
1 kilowatt (kw) = 1,000 watts = 1.3415 hp
 = 738 ft. lb./sec. = .948 Btu/sec. = 3,412 Btu/hr.
1 megawatt (MW) = 1,000 kilowatts (10^6 watts)
1 gigawatt (GW) = 1,000 megawatts (10^9 watts)
1 kw (capacity) = 8,760 kilowatthours (kwh) maximum
    annual production
1 kwh = 1.34 horsepower-hours (hph)
1 kwh = 3,412 Btu
1 kwh = 3.6 × 10^6 watt-seconds
 = 3.6 × 10^6 joules (3.6 megajoules)
1 kwh = 2.66 × 10^6 ft. lbs.
1 hp = 745.7 watts = 550 ft. lb./sec. = 2,544 Btu/hr.
1 watt-hour = 3.6 × 10^3 joules
1 Btu = 1,054 joules = .252 kcal = 778.3 ft. lb.

Energy Content of Fuel

1 lb of TNT = 478 kcal = 1,897 Btu
1 lb of bread = 1,300 kcal = 5,160 Btu
1 lb of wood = 1,800 kcal = 7,140 Btu
1 lb of crude oil (.14 gal) = 4,800 kcal = 19,000 Btu
1 lb of natural gas (25 ft^3) = 6,600 kcal = 26,000 Btu
bituminous coal = 24.8 million Btu/ton
gasoline = 5.25 million Btu/bbl
jet fuel (kerosene type) = 5.67 million Btu/bbl
wood and dry crop waste = 14-18 x 10^6 Btu/ton

	kwh	joules	calories	watt-years	Btu
1 kwh =	1	3.6×10^6	$.86 \times 10^6$	.114	3,410
1 joule =	$.278 \times 10^{-6}$	1	.239	31.7×10^{-9}	$.948 \times 10^{-3}$
1 calorie =	1.16×10^{-6}	4.18	1	13.3×10^{-6}	3.97×10^{-3}
1 watt-year =	8.77	31.6×10^6	7.54×10^6	1	29.9×10^3
1 Btu =	$.293 \times 10^{-3}$	1,054	252	33.4×10^{-6}	1
1 metric ton (10^6 g) anthracite coal yields	7,630	27.5×10^9	6.56×10^9	870	26×10^6
1 barrel of crude petroleum yields	1,641	5.91×10^9	1.41×10^9	187	5.6×10^6

Appendix D

ADDITIONAL SOLAR AND WIND DATA

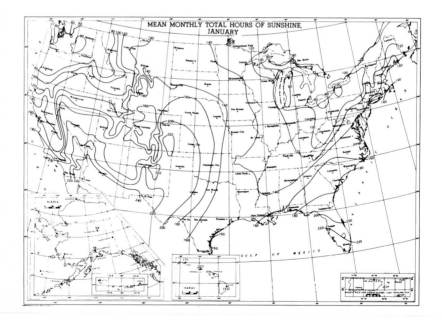

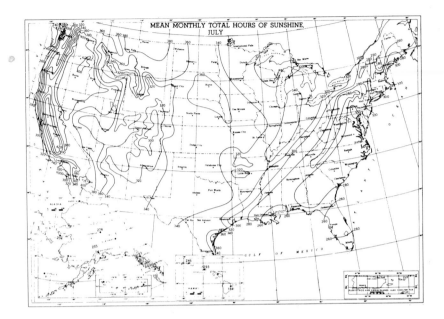

MEAN MONTHLY TOTAL HOURS OF SUNSHINE,
JULY

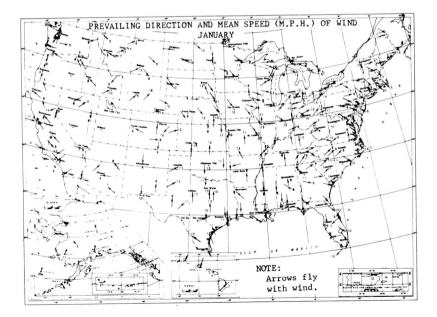

PREVAILING DIRECTION AND MEAN SPEED (M.P.H.) OF WIND
JANUARY

NOTE:
Arrows fly
with wind.

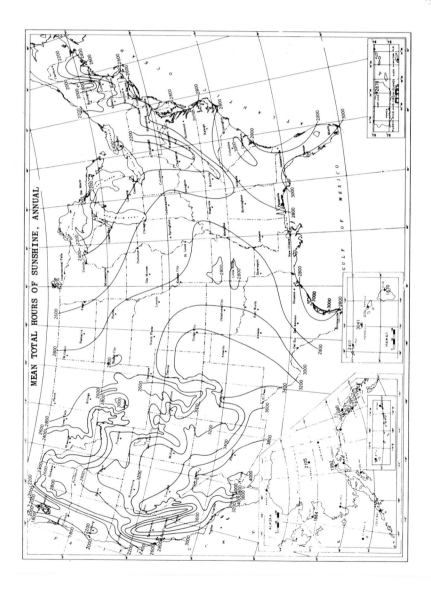

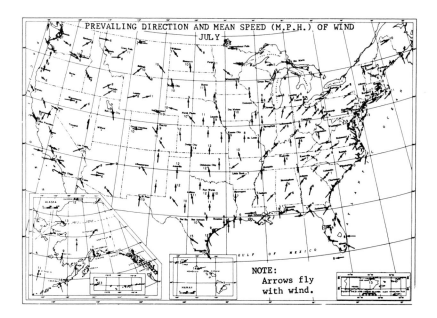

PREVAILING DIRECTION AND MEAN SPEED (M.P.H.) OF WIND
JULY

NOTE:
Arrows fly
with wind.

GLOSSARY

advection transfer of atmospheric properties, commonly heat by horizontal movements of air

air mass a body of air having similar properties of temperature and moisture

altimeter a barometer calibrated to indicate altitude instead of pressure

anabatic wind a wind which blows up a slope or mountain as the result of local surface heating

anemometer instrument which measures wind speed

anticyclone an area of high pressure

aphelion the point at which the orbit of the Earth takes it farthest from the Sun

Arctic sea smoke a fog formation resulting when very cold air crosses warm water

atmosphere envelope of air surrounding the earth

atmospheric pressure the force exerted by the weight of the atmosphere per unit area

barometer instrument for measuring atmospheric pressure. Two types are aneroid and mercurial.

barometric tendency changes in atmospheric pressure as sensed by a barometer

barrel a measure of volume equal to 42 gallons

Bermuda high semipermanent anticyclone in the Atlantic caused by downward flowing air of the general circulation

blizzard very cold, windy snow storm

British thermal unit (Btu) the amount of heat energy necessary to raise one pound of water by one degree Fahrenheit. Roughly the amount of heat produced by burning a wooden match completely (3412 Btu equal one kilowatt-hour).

Buys Ballot's Law If you stand with your back to the wind in the Northern Hemisphere, low pressure is to your left.

celsius temperature scale which is the same as Centigrade. 0° equals freezing point and 100° equals boiling point of water

chinook a warm, dry wind that blows down Rocky Mountain slopes

climate prevalent or characteristic meteorological conditions of a place or region

cloud visible cluster of minute water or ice particles above the earth's surface

cold front forward edge of an advancing cold air mass

condensation process by which a vapor becomes a liquid

condensation nuclei small particles in the air on which water vapor condenses, including but not limited to sea salt, pollution, and dust

conduction transfer of heat by molecular action in a material

contrail cloud-like streamer sometimes produced by aircraft exhaust as water vapor condenses in cold air

convection vertical air motion which transfers heat from lower to higher levels in the atmosphere

convergence condition that exists when air flows horizontally and collides with another air mass, resulting in the one flowing either over or under the other

coriolis force apparent force caused by the earth's rotation, which produces trajectories that curve to the right in the Northern Hemisphere

cumulonimbus cloud   a type of cloud with extensive vertical developments. Often a thunderstorm.

cyclone   an area of low atmospheric pressure that has a closed or circular circulation. Commonly called storms, cyclones are associated with vertical motion which produces inclement weather. Extratropical cyclones are accompanied by fronts and are denoted on maps by an L, or low. Tropical cyclones have no fronts and are often called hurricanes or typhoons.

degree-day   an approximate indication of the heating requirement for one day created by the mean outdoor temperature for that day. The number of degree-days added to the heating season by one day is equal to 65 degrees Fahrenheit minus the mean temperature for the day. For example, if the mean temperature for January 3rd is 35°F in a given location, that day adds 30 degree-days (65 – 35 = 30) to the year.

density   mass of a substance per unit volume.

dew   moisture condensed as liquid upon objects colder than the dew point of nearby air

dew point   temperature to which air must be cooled in order for saturation to occur

diurnal   daily, recurring every 24 hours

divergence   horizontal outflow of air from a location, resulting in vertical inflow from either above or below

drizzle   precipitation consisting of numerous tiny droplets usually associated with fog or low, nonvertically developed clouds

eddy   a whirl or circling current of air often associated with turbulent airflow

efficiency   the ratio of useful energy or work derived from a machine or process to the energy input, expressed as a percent

evaporation   transformation from a liquid to a gaseous state

Fahrenheit   temperature scale on which 32° denotes the freezing point and 212° the boiling point of water

fetch   length of open sea over which winds blow, creating waves

fog   a cloud at or near the earth's surface composed of numerous tiny droplets of water

fossil fuel coal, crude oil, or natural gas, the primary combustible substances formed over geological time spans by natural processes from the remains of plants and animals

front zone of transition between two different air masses

frost crystals of ice formed like dew, but below freezing

general circulation large scale air flow about the earth caused by unequal heating and cooling

geothermal energy the heat energy in the steam, heated water, or rocks beneath the earth's surface in many locations

glaze clear, smooth coating of ice which forms on objects when rain falls into cold air surrounding objects, or when raindrops are composed of water which is supercooled (below freezing)

greenhouse effect the warming of the earth's surface and lower atmosphere created by carbon dioxide and water vapor in the atmosphere, which absorb and reradiate infrared radiation

gust sudden increase in wind speed

hail precipitation which freezes in concentric layers about a core as vertical air currents drop and lift it. Most often found in thunderstorms.

halo luminous ring around sun or moon caused by ice crystals in the atmosphere

haze fine dust or salt particles which often attract water vapor and, when numerous, reduce visibility

high an area of high atmospheric pressure which has a closed circulation: an anticyclone

humidity the measure of water vapor content of the atmosphere

hurricane a tropical cyclone with speeds of 64 knots or greater

infrared the region of the electromagnetic spectrum consisting of radiation having a wavelength between approximately 700 nanometers (700 millimicrons, 7000 Angstroms) and 100,000 nanometers (100 micrometers).

insolation solar radiation received at the earth's surface

instability a state of the atmosphere in which the vertical distribution of temperature is such that a disturbance will cause a parcel of air to move away from its original location

inversion   a layer of air which is warmer than the air below it, inhibiting vertical motion

jet stream   a narrow, meandering stream of high speed wind embedded in the westerlies at higher altitudes

joule   A unit of energy. 1055 joules equal one Btu.

katabatic wind   airflow that moves downhill because the air is cold and dense

kinetic energy   The energy of an object in motion

land breeze   light wind that flows from land to sea during the night when land is cold and sea is warmer

langley   commonly used measure of solar radiation equal to one calorie of radiant energy per square centimeter. Solar radiation is often given in langleys per minute.

latent heat   1) of condensation: heat emitted when water vapor condenses to form water droplets. 2) of vaporization: heat absorbed by water and needed for a change of state to water vapor.

lightning. the sudden flash of light caused by electrical discharges in the atmosphere

low   an area of lower barometric pressure where air is rising, producing inclement weather: a cyclone, a storm

mean wind speed   average of wind speeds observed during a period of time

megawatt   One million watts, or one thousand kilowatts

mist   popular expression for drizzle

mountain wind   a light wind that blows downslope at night as the air is cooled; a katabatic wind

natural gas   a mixture of combustible hydrocarbon gases recoverable from the earth, mostly methane, having a chemical energy content of approximately 1000 Btu per cubic foot

nocturnal   occurring between sunset and sunrise

normal   average value of a meteorological element over a certain period of years

northeaster   a coastal storm which brings Northeast winds to the New England region

Orographic   in meteorology, an event caused by hilly or mountainous terrain

Perihelion That point at which the orbit of the Earth takes it closest to the Sun. It occurs about January 1st.

photovoltaic effect the conversion of sunlight directly into electricity by one of several solid state devices, such as a "silicon photovoltaic cell" or "solar cell"

polar air cold air formed in high northern latitudes

polar front the frontal zone between air masses of polar origin and those of tropical origin

polar high anticyclone formed when cold, dense air of the general circulation sinks near the pole

potential energy the ability of an object to do work by reason of its position or its configurations, for example, a massive object or a body of water that has been elevated, or a molecule that will liberate energy if its structure is changed.

power the rate at which energy is produced or work is done: for example, Btu per hour, joules per second (watts), or thousands of joules per second (kilowatts)

precipitation the name for moisture in liquid or solid form which falls from the atmosphere

pressure gradient change in atmospheric pressure per unit of horizontal distance

prevailing westerlies that part of the general circulation which flows from the west at mid—latitude

prevailing wind wind direction most frequently observed at a particular location

quad one quadrillion Btu's of energy

radiation energy transport by "shine." The warmth of sunshine through a window or of a glowing fire in a fireplace is heat generated primarily by radiation.

radiational cooling cooling of the earth and nearby air at night as heat is radiated to space

radiosonde a device containing meteorological instruments which is carried aloft by balloon and transmits data during ascension

rain shadow the area of lighter rainfall in the lee of a mountain

relative humidity ratio of the amount of moisture in the air to the amount which the air could hold at the same temperature if it were saturated, expressed as a percentage

renewable energy energy that recurs frequently compared to geological time scales

rime a type of icing formed by freezing of water droplets as they strike an exposed object. It is opaque and is often less formidable than glaze.

saturated air air that contains the maximum amount of water vapor it can hold at a given pressure and temperature. Its relative humidity is 100 percent.

sea breeze a light to moderate wind that flows from water to land during the day, driven by heating over the land

sea swell long, regular undulation of the sea surface generated by winds in a lengthy fetch

semipermanent high areas of descending air associated with the general circulation. Most often referring to oceanic highs near 30°N.

sensible heat the heat of a substance (such as a mass of water vapor) characterized by its temperature, as distinct from the heat it contains due to a change of phase. Water vapor may condense, for example, and liberate a relatively large amount of heat in the condensation process without a change in its temperature.

shower precipitation from vertically developed clouds characterized by sudden onset and demise, and rapid changes in intensity

smog a mixture of air pollution and fog commonly found in industrial areas and more recently discovered to be transported across regions

solar constant the earth's share of the sun's energy, received at the mean distance between earth and sun throughout the year. The best measurements put this quantity at 127.83 watts per square foot, or 436.19 Btu per hour per square foot, perpendicular to the sun's rays above the earth's atmosphere. Furthermore, this quantity is not really "constant". It varied by ±0.05 percent between November 1978 and May 1979 when measurements were conducted, and may have been quite different from its present value in earlier epochs.

solar energy the energy in sunshine. Measured on a horizontal plane at the earth's surface, this varies between 550 Btu per square foot per day in northern Europe to 2000 Btu per square foot per day in sunny deserts and most of the tropics.

solar spectrum electromagnetic energy from the sun with wavelengths between 0.3 and 3 millionths of a meter (micrometer)

source region an extensive area of the earth's surface which is uniform in meteorological conditions and imparts these values to an overlying air mass

squall line a narrow band of very active thunderstorms often preceding a cold front

stability state of the atmosphere in which the vertical distribution of temperature is such that an air parcel will resist displacement from its position

stationary front a zone between two different air masses which is not advancing and therefore is neither a cold or warm front.

storm usually referring to a low pressure area of marked intensity but also used to describe other types of disturbances such as thunderstorms and sandstorms

subsidence sinking motions of air, associated most often with high pressure, anticyclonic areas

thunderstorm an event produced by a cumulonimbus cloud and accompanied by lightning, thunder, rain, and sometimes by strong winds and hail

tornado violently rotating column of air defined by a funnel-shaped cloud of moisture and debris. It is usually associated with a cumulonimbus cloud, moves rapidly, and sometimes skips from place to place.

trade winds winds which blow from an easterly quadrant and are the southern periphery of the semipermanent oceanic highs, therefore part of the general circulation

trajectory path traced by an element in its movement over the earth's surface

tropical disturbance/depression a cyclonic wind system in the tropics which is not strong enough to be classified as a storm or hurricane

tropical air warm, humid air having its source in the tropical or subtropical latitudes

turbulence irregular motion of airflow produced by uneven surfaces or any intrusion into a smooth airflow

typhoon a severe tropical cyclone in the western Pacific, similar to a hurricane

valley wind   an airflow that moves from a valley upslope along a mountain during daytime when air is being heated; an anabatic wind

warm front   the forward edge of an advancing warm air mass at the earth's surface as the warmer air is being displaced upward over colder, more dense air

warm sector   the area where warm air is being compressed between an advancing cold front and retreating warm front

water vapor   moisture in the atmosphere which is gaseous and invisible

watt   a unit of power equal to one joule per second

watt hour   a unit of energy equal to one watt of power used continuously for one hour

weather   short-term variations of atmospheric temperature, pressure, wind, moisture, cloudiness, precipitation, and visibility

wind   horizontal motions of air

work   a force moving through a distance is said to do "work" in an amount equal to the product of the force times the distance, in appropriate units

BIBLIOGRAPHY

Anderson, Bruce, and Michael Riordan: *The Solar Home Book*, Brick House, Andover, MA, 1977.

Anthes, Richard, Hans Panofsky, John Cahir and Albert Rango: *The Atmosphere*, 2nd edition, Merrill Publishing Co., Columbus, Ohio 1978.

Bernard, Harold W., Jr.: *Weather Watch*, Ballinger, Cambridge 1979.

Commoner, Barry: *The Poverty of Power*, Alfred A. Knopf, New York, 1976.

Critchfield, Howard: *General Climatology,* 3rd edition, Prentice Hall, Englewood Cliffs, NJ, 1974.

Daniels, Farrington: *Direct Use of the Sun's Energy*, Yale University Press, New Haven, 1964.

Dorf, Richard C.: *Energy, Resources, and Policy*, Addison-Wesley, Reading, MA, 1978.

Duffie, John A., and William A. Beckman: *Solar Energy Thermal Processes*, John Wiley & Sons, New York, 1974.

225

Environmental Data Service: *Climatic Atlas of the U.S.*, U.S. Dept. of Commerce, ESSA, 1968. Reprinted by Environmental Data and Information Service, NOAA, 1979.

Gates, David: *Man and His Environment: Climate*, Harper & Row, New York 1972.

Glidden, William, Jr. and Colin High: *The New England Energy Atlas*, Resource Policy Center, Thayer School of Engineering, Dartmouth College, Hanover, NH, 1980.

Gilliam, Harold: *Weather of the San Francisco Bay Region*, University of Calif. Press, Berkeley, CA, 1962.

Hafele, Wolf, et al.: *Energy in a Finite World*, Ballinger, Cambridge, 1981.

Hammond, Allen L., et al.: *Energy and the Future*, American Association for Advancement of Science, Washington, D.C., 1973.

Hoecker, Walter: *Relative Effective Solar Space Heating over the U.S. Obtained from Southward-tilted Solar Collectors*, NOAA Technical Memorandum ERL ARL-73, Air Resources Laboratories, Silver Springs, MD, 1978.

Landsberg, Hans, et al.: *Energy: The Next Twenty Years*, Ballinger, Cambridge, 1979.

Lovins, Amory: "Energy Strategy: The Road Not Taken?" *Foreign Affairs*, October 1976, pp. 00.

Mazria, Edward: *The Passive Solar Energy Book*, Rodale Press, Emmaus, PA, 1979.

Petterssen, Sverre: *Introduction to Meteorology*, McGraw-Hill, New York 1941.

——: *Oceanography for Meteorologists*, 3rd edition, Prentice-Hall, New York, 1943.

Reed, Jack: *Wind Power Climatology of the U.S. (also supplement)*, Sandia Laboratories, Albuquerque, NM, 1977 (supplement 1979).

Stobaugh, Robert, and Daniel Yergin, ed.: *Energy Future*, Random House, New York, 1979.

Trewartha, Glenn, and Lyle Horn: *An Introduction to Climate*, 5th edition, McGraw-Hill, New York, 1980.

U.S. Government Printing Office: *The Atmosphere: Endangered and Endangering*, Washington, D.C., 1975.

Von Arx, William: *Introduction to Physical Oceanography*, Addison-Wesley, Reading, MA, 1962.

von Hippel, Frank, and Robert H. Williams: "Solar Technologies," *Bulletin of the Atomic Scientists*, November 1975, pp. 25-31.

Wegley, Harry, et al.: *A Siting Handbook for Small Wind Energy Conversion Systems*, Battelle Pacific Northwest Laboratories, Richland, WA, 1978.

Other energy related articles, *Solar Energy — The Journal of Solar Energy Science and Technology*, Pergamon Press, Parkville, Victoria, Australia, 1977-80.

INDEX